# The Last 3 Years

## OLIVIA OTTOLENGHI

**MILTON & HUGO L.L.C.**
4407 Park Ave., Suite 5
Union City, NJ 07087, USA

**Website:** *www. miltonandhugo.com*
**Hotline:** *1- 888-778-0033*
**Email:** *info@miltonandhugo.com*

Ordering Information:
Quantity sales. Special discounts are granted to corporations, associations, and other organizations. For more information on these discounts, please reach out to the publisher using the contact information provided above.

Library of Congress Control Number:      2025903499
ISBN-13:          979-8-89285-442-9      [Paperback Edition]
                  979-8-89285-441-2      [Digital Edition]

Rev. date: 01/31/2025

**For Myself, For Those Who've Loved and Lost, and For the Future**

*To the girl I was, navigating heartbreak and self-discovery; to those who've loved deeply, felt the pain of loss, yet found the courage to begin again; and to the future I'm building—one of hope, healing, and the love I know I deserve. May this journey remind us all that even in our darkest moments, there is always a way forward.*

# Authors Note

This book is a memoir—a personal reflection on the events and emotions of a relationship that brought me to this moment in my life. It is a raw and honest account of my journey through love, loss, and self-discovery. While deeply personal, I believe it reflects emotions and struggles that many of us face.

I've taken care to protect the privacy of those involved by changing names, locations, and identifying details, and certain moments have been dramatized for storytelling purposes.

I hope this book resonates with you—encouraging you to let go of what no longer serves you, inspiring you to choose your own happiness, and reminding you that you're not alone in navigating life's challenges. Thank you for allowing me to share my story with you.

# Contents

*Chapter*

*1*

# Where Paths Collide

Since I was a little girl, I always dreamed of finding "the one." Watching movies about love, I was captivated by the idea of soulmates—two people drawn together by a connection so deep it felt like fate. I believed my story would unfold like that someday. But before I met Austin, love felt more like a distant hope than a reality.

I had my heart broken by people who never truly cared for me. They weren't real relationships—more like fleeting moments of connection that left me feeling more alone than before. But those experiences shaped me. They taught me that I deserved more: more effort, more care, more love. So when I met Austin, I felt like all the disappointments had led me to something real.

Meeting Austin felt like discovering something I didn't even know I was missing. We connected through a dating app, and from our first conversation, there was an ease and familiarity I couldn't ignore. He wasn't like anyone I'd met before. He loved cars, just like my dad and brother, Nick, and we bonded over our shared dreams, our families, and the lives we hoped to build. With every message, I felt us growing closer, as though our hearts were aligning with each word.

One night, he asked me about the best date I'd ever been on. I paused, realizing I didn't have an answer. No one had ever taken me on a real date, and no one had ever brought me flowers. When I told him that, he seemed genuinely bothered, and he promised that our first date would be special. Over the next few weeks, we FaceTimed constantly, counting down the days until we could meet in person. It felt like the beginning of a story we were both eager to live.

The night finally came. Austin drove to my house, and before we left, he introduced himself to my family. He was nervous, but he wanted to make a good impression. Waiting for me in his truck was a bouquet of flowers—the first I'd ever received. My heart swelled as I held them, and I couldn't stop smiling. He took me to a fancy restaurant, the kind of place I'd only seen in movies. The dim lighting and soft music set the perfect tone, and as we talked, I felt completely at ease. Austin's smile lit up the room, and the way he looked at me made the world fade away.

After dinner, we walked back to his truck under the night sky, the air filled with a quiet excitement. He opened the door for me, a gesture that felt both sweet and intentional. As I settled into the seat, there was a moment of charged silence between us. He looked at me, his eyes soft and full of something I couldn't quite name. Before I could say anything, he leaned in and kissed me. It was gentle, almost hesitant, but it carried so much meaning—a promise of what was to come.

When he pulled back, he gave me a shy smile, and my heart raced. Warmth spread through me, and in that moment, everything felt right. We decided to head back to my house to watch a movie, but I could hardly focus on anything else. The night already felt perfect, like a dream I didn't want to wake from.

Inside, we barely paid attention to the movie, lost instead in conversation that stretched late into the night. My parents liked him immediately, which only made the night feel more special. Something shifted that night—a connection so real and profound that it felt like a turning point. We just clicked, and I knew I was falling for him. It was the kind of love I had always imagined, full of promise and possibility.

Even now, as I look back on that first night, I can't help but smile. It was the beginning of a love story I had always dreamed of—the kind that makes your heart race and your soul feel alive. For a while, it felt like the happily ever after I'd always hoped to find.

*Saturday, January 9, 2021*

*I don't think I'll ever forget tonight. I can still feel the butterflies from the way he looked at me, the way he held my gaze right before he kissed me. It was gentle and careful, almost as if he was as nervous as I was. But in that moment, everything felt right—like every piece of my life had been leading up to this.*

*He makes me feel seen, like he's genuinely listening to every word I say. I can talk to him about anything, from the silliest things to the dreams I never really share. Tonight, he met my family, and they all seem to like him. Watching my parents smile as they met him, seeing Nick and his girlfriend, Sophie, joke around with him— it made me feel like this could actually be something real.*

*I don't want to get ahead of myself, but I've never felt this way before. I've never had someone look at me the way he does, as if I'm important, as if he genuinely wants to be here. It scares me how much I want this to last, but for now, I'm just going to let myself enjoy it. Tonight, it feels like everything is possible with Austin.*

*Chapter*

# 2

# Snowfall and Sweet Beginnings

*Words Under the Stars*

The first few months with Austin felt like stepping into a dream. Every small gesture, every late-night conversation opened up a door to something new and thrilling. It was as if we were peeling back layers of ourselves, discovering parts we hadn't even known existed, all while weaving those pieces together into something that felt as if it had always been meant to be.

One night, just a few weeks in, we couldn't bear to wait until the weekend to see each other. It was a weeknight, but we decided to meet halfway in the parking lot of a small diner. The place was empty and quiet under the soft, gleaming streetlights. He pulled into the parking lot, and we both got out to greet each other. We climbed into his truck, not even thinking about going inside.

After what felt like hours of talking and debating whether or not to go inside, I laid across the bench seat of his truck. With my head on his lap, in the warmth of the heater, and George Strait playing from his radio. The night sky stretched out above us, dotted with stars. I remember the faint glow from the diner lights illuminating his face as he smiled at me. He reached over and tucked a loose strand of my hair behind my ear, his fingers lingering for just a moment. My heart fluttered, as a swarm of butterflies danced in my stomach, filling me with both excitement and nervousness.

"Do you realize," he said softly, "how crazy this all feels? How it feels like... I've known you forever?"

I laughed, looking down at my hands. "I was just thinking the same thing," I replied. "It's like... all of this is so easy, and I didn't expect it to be."

He took my hand, tracing small circles on my palm with his thumb. The gentle motion sent a shiver up my spine, and for a moment, I felt my heart race. I knew what I wanted to say, what had been bubbling up inside me for days. But voicing it felt like stepping off a ledge, as if saying it out loud would make everything real, vulnerable, raw.

Finally, I took a breath, the words spilling in a whisper. "Austin... I think I'm falling in love with you."

Before I could finish, he reached down, gently grabbing my face in his hands. His touch was so soft, yet so steady, that it took my breath away. He leaned in, his eyes locking onto mine, and in that moment, it was as if time stood still. The butterflies intensified, my stomach doing flips as he leaned closer, and before I could process it, he pressed his lips to mine. His kiss was slow, tender, like he was telling me everything he felt without saying a single word. It caught me off guard, but I melted into it, letting every unspoken feeling pour out in that one perfect moment.

When he pulled back, he kept his hands on my face, his thumbs gently brushing my cheeks as he looked into my eyes. "I love you too, Lily." he whispered, his voice steady, filled with a conviction that wrapped around me like a warm blanket. "I've been falling in love with you since the moment we met."

The butterflies in my stomach became a steady, joyful flutter as I realized this moment was everything I'd hoped for. The world outside faded away, and it was just the two of us, suspended in a moment that felt as if it had always been waiting for us to find it. A quiet sense of peace washed over me, grounding me in a way I'd never felt before. I could feel my heart pounding, my cheeks flushed, but for the first time, I felt like I didn't have to hold anything back.

We spent the rest of the night talking about everything we'd been afraid to say before. Our dreams, our fears, and the scars we both carried. He listened as I told him about the pain of past relationships, the heartbreaks that made me doubt I'd ever find someone who could truly love me. He didn't interrupt; he just held my hand, his thumb tracing gentle circles over my skin, his presence reassuring me with every word I spoke.

### Butterflies and Beginnings

With Valentine's Day approaching, I wanted to surprise him, to show him how much he meant to me. So I planned a trip to Hershey, hoping to give us a day of memories we could look back on. I knew how much he loved trucks, so I arranged for him to test-drive his dream truck at a dealership on the way to our first stop, and the look on his face was worth every second of planning.

"Are you serious?" he asked, looking at me in disbelief, his eyes wide with excitement.

I couldn't help but smile. "Only the best for you. Go on. Enjoy it."

He climbed behind the wheel, and for the next hour, I watched him come alive in a way I'd never seen before. Every smile, every laugh made my heart swell. We drove around the town, his hand resting on my knee, his thumb gently brushing over it. The butterflies returned, each small gesture from him reigniting that nervous excitement.

Our first stop was a cozy little breakfast spot in Lancaster, a place I knew from family trips over the years. Sharing it with him felt intimate like I was inviting him into a part of my past, and seeing him there made it feel like I was creating a new memory with someone who truly mattered.

Later, we wandered through the butterfly atrium at the Hershey Gardens, taking in the beauty of the flowers and the butterflies flitting around us. Ever so often, he'd reach out and point to a butterfly, his face lighting up with childlike wonder. Each small moment, each laugh and smile added to the quiet magic of the day. We strolled through the grounds of the Hershey Hotel, our footsteps soft in the fresh winter air, and it felt like a fairytale, like the beginning of a story I never wanted to end.

### Asking for Forever

After our adventure, we ended the night curled up in my parent's basement, watching movies as snow began to fall outside. The blizzard was in full force, but we didn't care. The world outside could've disappeared, and I wouldn't have minded as long as he was there beside me. We sat close, but something about his silence, the way he kept glancing at me, felt different. He seemed nervous, like he was holding something back.

It was around two am, he turned to me, his expression serious, but with a hint of vulnerability I hadn't seen before. "I have something I want to ask you," he murmured, his voice barely above a whisper. My heart raced, the butterflies stirring wildly as he reached for my hands, holding them in his as he took a deep breath. "What is it?" I whispered, my voice just as soft, the anticipation almost overwhelming.

He looked down at our joined hands, his thumb brushing over my knuckles, before lifting his gaze to meet mine. His eyes held a mixture of excitement and nervousness. "Will you be my girlfriend?"

The words hung in the air, heavy with meaning. It was the question I hadn't realized I'd been waiting for, the one that made everything feel real, solid. I felt a smile spread across my face, and without a moment's hesitation, I whispered, "Finally... Yes, Austin."

My heart fluttered with joy, filling me with the certainty that this was exactly where I was meant to be. He leaned in, capturing my lips in a kiss, one that sealed the beginning of something I knew was special.

### Love and Snowfall

The next morning, I woke up to the world covered in a soft blanket of white, the snow still falling gently outside the window. The excitement was impossible to contain; I ran downstairs to wake Austin. "It's so pretty outside. Do you want to go out and drive around, maybe take some pictures together?"

He smiled, nodding. "I'd love that."

We spent the morning driving through empty roads, everything quiet and blanketed in white. At one point, we pulled into a park and got out to take pictures. As we stood there in the gentle snowfall, he wrapped his arms around my waist, pulling me close. We both looked up at the sky as the snowflakes fell, and in that perfect, quiet moment, he looked into my eyes and whispered, "I love you so much."

As the butterflies returned to my stomach, I felt the warmth of his words. He leaned down, pressing his lips softly to mine, and for that moment, everything was quiet, still, and perfect – just him, me, and the snow falling around us.

### Sunday, February 7, 2021

*I still can't believe that night happened. I've replayed it in my head a hundred times already, and each time, it feels just as surreal as it did in the moment. I didn't know love could feel like this – so all-consuming and pure. When I looked at Austin, every doubt I had about opening up again just melted away. It was like the world around us faded, and all I could see was him, his eyes, and that soft smile that makes me feel like everything is exactly as it should be.*

*I was so nervous to say the words, even though I knew it was true. When I finally managed to get out, "I'm falling in love with you," his reaction made my heart skip. Before I could even take a breath, he was there, holding me close, telling me he felt the same. I could feel it in the way he looked at me, as if I was the only person who mattered. And when he kissed me… that's a moment I'll hold on to forever.*

*Last night was amazing, just the two of us. It felt like the most sincere way to ask me to be his girlfriend. This morning was just as perfect– the snow still falling gently as we walked together, laughing, taking pictures, capturing this moment of pure happiness. When he pulled me close at the park and told me he loved me again, everything felt complete. I didn't know it was possible to feel so safe with someone.*

*I know it's early, and I'm getting ahead of myself, but I don't think I've ever felt this way. I've been hurt before, and I know the risks. But with Austin, it's different. For the first time, I don't feel like I have to hold anything back. I feel free to be myself, to share everything – even the parts of me I've always tried to protect. He makes me feel like maybe, just maybe, love really can last.*

*Chapter*

3

# Bridging Two Worlds

From the beginning, Austin and I connected in a way that felt like magic—an instant spark that made the hours fly by during our FaceTime calls. Living an hour apart meant we couldn't see each other daily, so those late-night conversations became our lifeline, the way we stayed close despite the distance. Over the screen, we became best friends, talking about our days, sharing laughs, and little pieces of our worlds. It didn't matter that I was in Pennsylvania and he was in Delaware; the screen bridged the miles, allowing us to build something special before we even had our first date.

But there were subtle reminders that Austin and I came from two very different worlds. My life was centered around a big, close-knit family that celebrated every birthday, marked every holiday, and supported each other through everything. My parents were together, and family was my comfort zone. In my family, there was a natural openness—we shared the good and the bad with each other. It wasn't about being perfect, but about feeling connected and supported. I always felt like I could be myself and share whatever was on my mind.

Austin's world was different. His parents had divorced, and he grew up with his mom and stepdad in a quieter, more independent way. There wasn't the same kind of closeness or open sharing that I was used to. I noticed that he kept parts of his life to himself, guarded and hesitant, as if there were parts of him always just out of reach. At times, it made me feel like I was constantly trying to get to know him, peeling back the layers that he'd closed off, hoping he'd let me in completely.

I wanted to bridge the gap between our families, to make him feel as welcome in mine as I wanted to feel in his. But Austin didn't see it that way. He was private in a way I wasn't, and my habit of calling my parents to share little things—whether it was about my day or something we had done—became a source of tension.

One weekend, I called my mom while Austin and I were at his house. She had the day off, and since her work hours often kept us apart, weekends were one of the few chances I had to check in. It was just a quick call, but when I hung up, Austin gave me a sharp look.

"What?" I asked, already sensing the frustration behind his silence.

He leaned back against the counter, crossing his arms. "Do you really have to call them all the time? We're supposed to be spending the weekend together, but you're always on the phone."

I stared at him, confused. "It was five minutes, Austin. I just wanted to say hi and check in."

He rolled his eyes, pushing off the counter. "You don't see me calling my parents 24/7, do you? It's like you can't go a single day without telling them something."

"It's not like that," I said, trying to stay calm. "She's my mom. I don't see her as much during the week because of work, so I check in on weekends. It's not a big deal."

"To you, maybe," he muttered under his breath, grabbing his phone. "It's just... weird."

"Weird?" I echoed, feeling my patience slip. "Why is it weird to call my mom?"

He sighed, clearly annoyed. "It's not just that. You're always telling them things about me. Why do they need to know every little thing I do?"

I hesitated, trying to find the right words. "Because I'm proud of you. When you tell me something good, I want to share it. I want them to see what I see in you."

He shook his head, a bitter laugh escaping his lips. "I don't need them to be proud of me, Lily. It's my life. I don't even tell my own parents this stuff."

"Well, maybe you should," I shot back before I could stop myself. "They might want to know."

"Whatever," he muttered, turning away. "It's just annoying."

It wasn't the first time we had this conversation, and it wouldn't be the last. The frustration always felt one-sided; I couldn't understand why something so small—so normal to me—bothered him so much. I didn't call my parents to exclude him or take away from our time. I just wanted to stay connected to the people who meant the most to me, and I wanted him to feel like a part of that.

As our relationship blossomed, Austin seemed open, warm, and eager to build something meaningful with me. I remembered how he would open doors for me, always show affection, and make me feel like the center of his world. In those early days, he was the kind of person I had dreamed of finding. He'd tell me how much he loved me, how much he cherished our time together. Those were the moments that reassured me that this was real, that we were building something solid together.

But over time, something shifted. It wasn't sudden, more like a slow drift that crept in over months, a rollercoaster of ups and downs. Austin became more closed off, pulling away in ways that were gradual but undeniable. Where he had once shared everything with me, he began to shut down, keeping more to himself, leaving me wondering what had changed. I'd find myself lying awake after our calls, replaying conversations in my mind, trying to pinpoint the exact moment things started to change, questioning if I'd done something wrong.

At first, I convinced myself it was my fault—that if I could just be a better girlfriend, if I tried harder, I could bring us back to the closeness we once had. But it was like trying to hold water in my hands; no matter how tightly I tried to hold on, it kept slipping through my fingers. He'd have moments of quietness that he'd describe as "calm," but it felt different—a subtle tension, an edge to his words that hinted at something else. His mom would brush it off, calling it his "man period," but it felt more complex, especially when that edge was directed at me.

There were times he'd go silent, his face hard to read, and I'd feel like I was talking to a stranger rather than the person I'd grown so close to. The "I'm fine" responses and shrugged-off answers became a painful refrain in our relationship, a barrier I couldn't break through no matter how hard I tried. His frustration or moodiness would come and go, creating a cycle of calm followed by tension, a pattern that led to countless arguments where I felt I was trying to hold onto something slipping away.

I wanted to so badly bridge the distance between us—not just the physical miles but the emotional space that was starting to form. Yet, I couldn't ignore the feeling that he was searching for something else, something I couldn't give. That undercurrent of tension between us, the feeling of constantly chasing an elusive closeness, became a weight on my heart. For every sweet moment that we shared, there was a growing sense of unease, a question that lingered: was I enough for him?

In those early days, he made me feel like we were unstoppable, like love could conquer anything. But now, that love was beginning to feel like a fragile thing I was constantly trying to protect. I could still remember those nights of talking endlessly, the way he'd make me laugh and feel special, the way he'd look at me like I was the only person in the world. I held onto this foundation for the entirety of our relationship, clinging to the person he was in the beginning. The one I so blindly clung to, that dragged me through the spiral of what was the last three years.

### Sunday, July 11, 2021

*I can't shake this feeling that something's changing between us. Maybe it's nothing—just a rough patch, or maybe he's just stressed. But sometimes, it feels like he's slipping away, and I don't know what to do about it. He tells me he loves me, and I believe him. I feel it, too, in the quiet moments when it's just us, when he's so close, so affectionate, like he truly wants to be here.*

*Most of the time, he's warm and attentive, making me feel like I'm the center of his world. But every now and then, it's as if a switch flips, and suddenly he's different—distant, annoyed, almost like being around me is a chore. I can't always predict when it'll happen; it's like he just slips into this mood without warning. When I ask him if everything is okay, he shrugs it off, saying he's just in a "calm mood." But I know the difference between calm and something else. I just can't figure out what that "something else" is.*

*Maybe I'm overthinking it. Maybe I'm the one who's making it bigger than it is. But every time he goes quiet, every time he's just out of reach, I feel like I'm losing him piece by piece. I wish he'd let me in and let me understand what's going on in his head. I keep wondering if I've done something wrong, if maybe I'm just not enough to keep him here. It's like I'm holding onto something that's slowly slipping through my fingers.*

*I want to believe that this will pass, that things will go back to the way they were when we first met, when everything felt so simple and easy. I miss that version of us, the one that laughed and stayed up talking about our dreams like there was no tomorrow. Now, it feels like he's already halfway gone, and I'm scared that one day, he won't come back.*

*But I'm not ready to give up on us. Not yet. Maybe tomorrow will be better. Maybe he just needs time, and things will be okay again. I hope I'm right. I need to be right.*

*Chapter*

# 4

# Family Ties

From the very beginning, my relationship with Austin's mom, Pam, was a source of comfort and warmth. She welcomed me into her life with open arms, always making me feel seen and appreciated. We shared more than just surface-level conversations, and in her, I found someone who genuinely valued the way I cared for her son. She loved how I supported him, looked after him, and expressed my love in ways she admired. In many ways, it felt like she recognized things in me that I wished Austin would see, and having her acknowledge that meant the world.

Over time, Pam and I became close friends as much as family. She even encouraged me to work part time with her, opening doors that would eventually lead to my internship. When Austin was busy, she'd invite me over. We'd go on ice cream dates, do our nails together, shop, or play board games. When Austin wanted to be alone, I'd join his family upstairs, sharing stories, laughing, and feeling like I genuinely belonged in their home.

His stepdad, Bill, was equally kind—a quiet man with a warm heart who felt like an additional father figure in my life. It was clear to me that he was Austin's true father figure, always invested in his happiness and well-being.

Austin's grandparents were also part of this extended circle that made our relationship feel even stronger. His mom's parents were welcoming, and his grandmother's affectionate hugs became a comforting gesture. His dad's parents, too, reminded me of my own grandparents, whom I had lost too soon. Spending time with them was nostalgic and meaningful, and I often encouraged Austin to cherish these family moments, knowing how precious they were.

On my side, Austin fit in seamlessly with my dad and brother. Bonding over cars, they would spend hours talking, laughing, and sharing stories. When he visited, he and my dad would sit together, watching car auctions on TV and discussing their favorite models, as though he was already part of our family. Those connections felt natural and fulfilling.

My mom, however, never quite clicked with Austin. She's one of the kindest people I know, deeply caring about everyone in her life, but Austin always seemed wary of her openness. He believed she didn't like him, though I knew she only wanted to see me happy. While my dad and brother's relationships with Austin flourished effortlessly, I could sense the quiet disappointment in my mom. She wanted to feel that same connection, but Austin seemed indifferent, focusing on my dad and brother instead. I wanted him to fully embrace my family, and it hurt to know he wasn't making an effort with her.

There were moments when my mom tried to bring her concerns to me. I can still hear her careful tone during one of those conversations.

"Why is he always on his phone when he's here?" she asked one evening after Austin had gone home. Her voice was soft, but there was no mistaking the concern behind it.

I sighed, already feeling defensive. "Mom, he's just comfortable here. It's not a big deal."

She raised an eyebrow, crossing her arms. "Comfortable? He's sitting on the couch on his phone while the rest of us are at the table having a conversation. That's not comfortable—that's rude."

"Mom, he's just not used to big family conversations. It's overwhelming for him," I argued, trying to downplay her concern.

Her lips pressed into a thin line. "Overwhelming or not, he's here with you. He should be making an effort. Does he act like this with his own family?"

That question stung, but I quickly brushed it off. "It's different. He's just shy. You know how people are when they're in new environments."

She gave me a long, searching look. "He's not new here anymore. I've been trying to get to know him, but every time I ask him something, it's like pulling teeth. He doesn't go beyond surface-level answers. Don't you think that's strange?"

I shook my head, frustrated. "That's just how he is, Mom. You're reading too much into it."

Her expression softened, but her words didn't. "I just don't want you to ignore the red flags because you care about him so much. You deserve someone who wants to be part of your life—your whole life."

Looking back, I wish I had listened more. I always rushed to defend him, convinced she didn't understand him the way I did. But deep down, I knew she was right. Austin rarely put in the effort to bond with her. He clung to me at family events, never straying far enough to have more than a passing conversation with anyone else. It left me feeling trapped, constantly aware of the tension between them. I never felt comfortable leaving him alone, afraid he'd isolate himself or say something dismissive that would only widen the gap.

We had another conversation after a particularly tense dinner. Austin had spent most of the evening scrolling through his phone while my mom tried to draw him into the conversation.

Later, she pulled me aside. "Why does he act like that?" she asked, her voice tinged with frustration. "I'm trying to include him, but he doesn't seem interested."

"He's just tired," I replied weakly. "He's had a long day."

She frowned. "We all have long days, but we still show up. He's dating you. He should care about being here and connecting with your family."

"Mom, you're being too hard on him," I snapped, feeling cornered.

Her face fell, and I immediately regretted my tone. "I'm not trying to hurt you," she said quietly. "I just want you to think about what this says about how much he values you and your family."

Her words lingered long after the conversation ended, but I wasn't ready to face the truth she was gently trying to show me.

As time went on, my mom and I started having disagreements about Austin. They weren't explosive fights, but the tension between us was undeniable. If she tried to bring something up, I'd cut her off or get defensive, which only made her pull away. I hated the way we'd tiptoe around each other after those moments, the silence stretching between us like a chasm.

She would become distant, and I would overcompensate, trying to prove to her that Austin was good, that our relationship was solid. But the truth was, her concerns lingered in the back of my mind, even when I wouldn't admit it.

Now, looking back, I owe my mom an apology. She saw the cracks long before I did, and she tried—time and time again—to bring them to my attention. I brushed her off, defended him, and in doing so, I put a strain on our relationship. She didn't deserve that. She was only trying to protect me, to guide me, and I fought her every step of the way.

I wish I had listened. I wish I had trusted her intuition. Maybe things would have been different. Maybe I wouldn't have felt so alone in carrying the weight of a relationship that was slowly breaking me.

To my mom, I'm sorry—for the arguments, the distance, and for not seeing then what I see so clearly now. You were right, and I should have let you in, instead of pushing you away.

In so many ways, our connections with each other's families kept me committed to Austin for longer than I could have imagined. Pam was like a second mother, and her acceptance and belief in my love for Austin filled me with hope during the challenging times. Despite his distant relationship with my mom, I kept believing things would improve. I thought the love we shared with each other's families would be enough to bridge the gaps that were forming between us.

Yet, even as we grew closer to each other's families, there were hints of something else—the same quiet tension, a distance that occasionally surfaced. It would come and go like a shadow, sometimes briefly pulling Austin away, leaving me questioning what I might have done wrong. And then, just when I thought we were settling into a life surrounded by family and love, Kayla appeared. Her presence marked a subtle shift—a hint of something hidden, the first sign of a silence in Austin that felt heavier than usual. The bonds of family felt strong, yet they couldn't hold together the cracks that were beginning to form as Austin seemed to drift further into his own world.

# *Chapter*

# 5

# Secrets and Second Chances

### The First Red Flag

Kayla was Austin's first friend to follow me on social media. When the request came through, I glanced at him, phone in hand. "Who's Kayla?" I asked, showing him the screen.

"Oh, she's just an old friend from high school," he replied with a shrug. "We don't really talk anymore."

"Alright," I said, brushing it off. If he wasn't concerned, I figured I shouldn't be either. I accepted her request and thought nothing of it, not knowing that she'd be the first to set off a gut feeling that would follow me for the next three years.

That feeling crept up on me again later that summer. Austin was at my house, and, as usual, he drank too much. When he started stumbling, I brought him inside to help him to bed. As I ran upstairs to grab his phone, my heart nearly stopped when a notification lit up the screen–an Instagram message from someone named "Stella" on a different account he'd created. The message preview read, "I promise I won't say anything to her."

A wave of nausea filled through me. I didn't know this feeling yet, but something deep down told me to read more. I opened the message, and my heart sank further. I scrolled. Stella had sent him photos, inappropriate ones, and there he was, replying, "Just don't say anything to my girlfriend, Please."

I continued scrolling, almost against my will at this point. Their conversations were riddled with attempts to figure out who the other was, both hiding behind these "fake" Instagram accounts. Message after message, they guessed, teased, and probed until the truth finally came out—they admitted it to each other. Stella wasn't some random girl; Stella was Kayla.

The pit in my stomach grew deeper, almost unbearable. He had been hiding this side of him, and it broke me. I went downstairs, trying to keep my hands from shaking, and shoved the phone in his face. "What is this, Austin?" I demanded. "You're messaging Kayla on a fake account?"

He blinked at the screen, his face turning pale, then dropped his head to his hands. "I don't know... I didn't think it would mean anything," he mumbled. "My dad... he cheated on my mom. I hate that he did that to her, and I promised myself I'd never be like him. I've never done anything like this before. I don't know what got into me... it was just this stupid, impulsive thing, and now I feel sick about it. I hate myself for doing this to you."

It was hard to reconcile the hurt he'd caused me with the pain in his voice. A part of me wanted to believe him. We were still so new, so fresh into dating. I took a shaky breath, nodded slowly, and whispered, "Fine. But this is it, Austin. I'm serious. I can't do this if you're going to lie to me."

Months passed, and I tried to let go of what had happened, to trust him again. But that feeling in my stomach–the one that told me something was off–stayed with me. It didn't always flare up, but it was there, lying dormant, just waiting for another message, another slip-up to bring it back.

## *Thanksgiving Rumors*

Then, around Thanksgiving, I was with my grandmother at a doctor's appointment when my phone rang. It was Austin, calling me in the middle of his workday–something he never did.

"Hey," I answered, stepping outside the office. "Is everything okay?"

"I… need to tell you something," he began, his voice tight. "Jacob told me that Morgan ran into Kayla last night, and she started saying all this stuff about me."

My stomach dropped, that same pit returning. "What stuff?"

"She told Morgan that we've been talking for a while, that we reconnected on Tinder," he said quickly. "She even said I'm not happy with you and want to be with her."

"What?" I could barely get the word out, my voice shaking. "Is any of it true, Austin?"

"Of course not!" he replied, sounding almost hurt that I'd ask. "Kayla's crazy. She always had a crush on me in high school, and now she's making stuff up. She's just jealous."

I paused, trying to read between the lines. "Are you sure? Because she's saying some pretty specific things, and you've talked to her before behind my back."

He sighed. "She's lying, Lily. Block her, I'll block her too. This way, she's out of our lives for good."

I agreed, but the nagging feeling stayed with me, that same pit in my stomach I'd had when I first saw her messages. Still, I told myself to let it go and moved on.

## *A New Year's Betrayal*

A year later, I'd almost forgotten about Kayla. She'd been out of the picture, or so I thought. But then, on New Year's Eve of 2022, everything came crashing down.

Austin and I celebrated the holiday at my brother's house, and, as usual, he got blackout drunk. When we got home, I put him to bed and went to relax in my room. A few minutes later, I noticed he'd opened a Snapchat I'd sent him earlier.

I texted him, "Honey, I thought you were going to sleep? You okay?" No answer.

That pit in my stomach quickly returned, stronger than ever. I walked into the guest room and found him passed out, his phone laying open to a conversation with… Kayla. My heart sank as I saw her name on the screen. He was too drunk to wake up, so I took his phone to my room and opened the conversation, and without a single thought and filled with rage, I started texting back.

"What were we talking about again?" I typed, the words coming almost instinctively.

Her reply came quickly. "About how you wanted to take me out if you ever break up with Lil. And how you've been saying you'll do it for months but never do."

Lil… Lil? She's calling me Lil? I have never spoken to this chick in my entire life. I never even met her, let alone know her well enough to be calling me Lil. My hands shook as I read her message. I typed again, "Right… when was this?"

"A few weeks ago," she replied, as if it were the most natural thing in the world.

I turned off his phone, set it down, and lay awake, tears streaming down my face as the familiar ache settled in. I thought about waking him, confronting him then and there, but he was beyond drunk; he would never wake up. I'd deal with it in the morning.

The next day, as soon as he heard me moving, Austin came to my door.

I opened the door, anger and hurt radiating through me. The look on his face said it all–he knew. "Lily," he whispered, his voice crackling. "I can explain."

"Explain?" I shot back. "You lied to me. After everything you put me through with her… you promised me she was out of your life."

He tried to take my hand, but I pulled back and sat on the bed. "Please, Lily. I know I messed up, but let me make it up to you. Let me prove to you that I'm serious."

"Prove it?" I echoed, the frustration bubbling over. "You've told me that before, and yet here we are. If you're serious, then sit down right now and tell her that it's over, that you never want to hear from her again."

He hesitated for a moment, then sat down on the bed beside me, his face pale as he reached for his phone. I watched as he opened their conversation, and it felt surreal–like I was having an out-of-body experience, watching this unfold. I had never thought in my life that I would be telling a man to text another woman that he wanted to be with me. I never imagined I'd be in this situation, where I'd have to force someone to prove their loyalty in such a humiliating way.

His fingers hovered over the screen, and he glanced at me, but I didn't let him waver. "Text her," I said, my voice steely. "Tell her you don't know what you were thinking, that you love me and only me, and that you two can't talk anymore.

I watched him type the message, each word feeling like a small, bitter victory. It was satisfying, but it hurt all the same. When he hit send, I felt a mixture of relief and emptiness, as if something fundamental had changed between us.

I didn't know if I could ever fully trust him again. But for that moment, I continued to stay, telling myself that maybe this time, he'd fully understand the cost of his choices.

*Chapter*

# 6

# Friends and Favors

### Building Connections

From the beginning, Austin's friends played a big part in our relationship. His best friend, Jacob, and his fiance, Amber, were the first of Austin's friends that I met, and they quickly became a regular presence in our lives. Jacob and Austin were inseparable–Jacob was like a brother to him, they worked together and were partners in just about everything. Together, they'd share everything, from late-night talks to plans for the weekend.

I first met Jacob and Amber at Austin's house. They had a nine-month-old daughter, Maisy, and being the caring person that I am, I immediately made an effort to connect with them. I took photos at Maisy's birthday parties, bought gifts for her even when it wasn't her birthday, and would often take Amber and Maisy out for lunch. Amber didn't work, and Jacob would often complain about money, so I'd pay for us on those outings. We went to the zoo, played games with Maisy, and did little outings, always on my dime. I never asked for anything in return, after all, that's what friends do.

We spent nearly every weekend with Jacob and Amber. We'd go to concerts, out for dinner, festivals, and parties together. I built a unique bond with Jacob, one that felt almost like a sibling relationship. We'd pick on each other to the point that everyone else just ignored us because it had become a regular occurrence.

### A Sudden Rift

A little over two years into my relationship with Austin, things took a turn. One night, we were hanging out in Jacob and Amber's garage, as usual. Jacob and I were throwing a bouncy ball back and forth, messing around, when I accidentally knocked his beer out of his hand, spilling it all over his shirt. It was as if a switch flipped. Suddenly, Jacob was furious. He stormed over, grabbed my chair, and shoved me across the garage floor.

Everyone turned to watch, stunned. I was shocked that he'd gotten so upset over a spilled beer, especially since it had always been part of our playful dynamic. I apologized, saying it was just a beer and could easily be washed out, but he called me a bitch and stormed out of the garage. For a moment, no one spoke. Finally, I looked at Austin and said, "I'm ready to leave."

As we walked outside, Jacob came back up the driveway. I tried to talk to him, hoping to smooth things over. "Are you seriously this upset over something so small?"

"It is a big deal," he snapped, "and I don't care if you never come back here again." "Why would you say that?" I asked, trying to understand where this was coming from. "This isn't going to change our friendship, right?"

"I don't care about you," he said coldly. "Austin's my best friend, and that'll never change. But you? I don't care."

Austin and I got into his truck, and he drove us away in silence. I started to cry, but Austin just kept his eyes on the road. "Are you mad at me?" I asked, confused and hurt.

"You shouldn't have been messing around with him in the first place," he replied, almost dismissively.

For weeks after, everyone was walking around on eggshells. Jacob and Austin kept talking daily, and the whole incident was swept under the rug. Finally, I decided to be the bigger person. I texted Jacob, asking if we could talk. He called, and I apologized again, saying I didn't want this to affect my relationship with Austin or their friendship. He brushed it off, saying it was fine, but things still felt tense and distant. We didn't see them as often, and I was still hurt that Austin hadn't stood up for me.

### Birthday Disappointments

A few weeks later, it was my 21st birthday, and I wanted to celebrate with our friends. We went to Dave & Buster's—a place where we could drink and enjoy activities with the kids. I spent the night hanging out with my friend Kate but occasionally checked in with Amber and Maisy, who wound up disappearing halfway through the night, and when we found them near the entrance, Amber seemed off. When I asked if something was wrong, she insisted it was nothing.

When Austin and I got home, Jacob texted him, saying that he and Austin needed to talk because Amber felt I was ignoring her and leaving her out. I explained that it was my birthday and I had tried to include her, but I couldn't follow her around the whole night. It felt childish that she'd complain to Jacob instead of talking to me directly.

A couple days later, Amber texted me, saying she felt like I wasn't close to her anymore and that Maisy was the only person she felt connected to. I told her I'd always been there for her and Maisy, and how hurt I was that she hadn't reached out to me when things got tense with Jacob. Things never really felt the same after that.

For Austin's birthday, I planned a surprise gathering at a brewery he loved. Only Kate, her boyfriend, and one of Austin's coworkers showed up. The rest of them made excuses but invited Austin out to celebrate on a weeknight when they knew I wouldn't be there. Eventually, Austin stopped reaching out to Jacob, and though Jacob tried to reconnect, Austin kept his distance.

### Words Left Unspoken

One night, Austin received a Facebook message from Jacob's mom, reminding him that he was Maisy's godfather and that he was setting a bad example by distancing himself from their family. She claimed that I was the reason he wasn't coming around and that a "true friend" would never allow a relationship to interfere.

In the end, the friendship faded. At a mutual friend's wedding, Austin and Jacob acted like nothing happened, but Amber made it clear how she felt. By the end of the night, she pulled me aside, drunkenly saying, "I don't really want to be around you right now."

"I feel the same way," I replied and walked away.

I'll never understand why Austin never stood up for me. I went out of my way for his friends, especially for Maisy, because I wanted him to see how much I cared. I thought that by showing him I valued his friendships, he'd see how serious I was about our relationship and how committed I was to building a future together. I poured myself into trying to make a place for myself within his world, hoping he'd one day stand up for me with the same conviction.

But after everything, I was left wondering if it was all for nothing. It hurt to think that I'd done so much–organizing parties, going out of my way for his friends, treating them like family–only to realize that, when things got tough, they'd shut me out, and he'd let them. Even after the distance set in, Austin never addressed it, never defended me, never reassured me that I was worth more than their approval.

As time went on, I tried to let go of the hurt. I kept telling myself that it wasn't my fault, that I'd done my best to be there for him and his friends, and maybe that was all I could do. Still, the disappointment lingered, a constant reminder that the relationship I had invested so much in could be one-sided.

In quiet moments, I'd catch myself wondering: would he ever truly be able to choose me? Or was I destined to always feel like an outsider, always trying to prove myself, always hoping that one day, he'd see me the way I'd seen him all along–worth fighting for?

That realization sat heavy with me, adding to the doubts that had begun to gather. It became clearer with each passing day that the friendships I had fought to nurture were never really mine. And maybe, in a way, Austin wasn't truly mine either.

## Friday, March 10, 2023

*I can still feel the sting of Jacob's words echoing in my head. I keep replaying that moment in the garage, the way he shoved me over a spilled beer, like that's all it took for him to show how little he thinks of me. And then he looked me in the eyes and told me he didn't care if I was ever around again. All I could think was, after everything I've done for you, for Maisy, for Amber... this is what I get?*

*But it's not just Jacob—it's Austin's reaction, or really, his lack of one, that hurts even more. On the drive home, he barely said a word, like this was my fault somehow. I was hoping for a sign, any sign, that he was upset about how I'd been treated. But instead, I felt like I was the one walking on eggshells, afraid to push too hard or expect too much.*

*I even asked him, "Are you mad at me?" And his response... "You shouldn't have been messing around with him in the first place." I keep asking myself why I'm putting so much energy into this, why I'm the one who's always bending and forgiving and trying. I've done everything to support his friendships, showing up for his friends and family as if they were my own, thinking it would show him how serious I am about us. But tonight, I'm starting to wonder if any of it means anything to him.*

*I just don't know how much longer I can keep fighting for a place in his life when he won't fight for me. I went out of my way for Jacob and Amber, not because I had to, but because I wanted to—because they mean something to him, and by extension, they meant something to me. But now I feel like a stranger all over again, and Austin's silence tells me that's exactly how he's okay with things staying.*

*Tonight, I feel so alone. I wonder if this is just going to be the pattern forever—me pouring in, him taking it for granted, and never knowing if I'll ever be the one he'll finally stand up for.*

*Chapter*

# 7

# Falling Into Him

From the very beginning, Austin had a way of making me feel as though I was the only person in his world. There was a connection between us that felt electric, but it wasn't just his touch or his words. It was how he looked at me, how he held me, how he made me feel seen in a way I hadn't known was possible. His presence, his intensity—it all drew me in, and before I knew it, I was lost in him.

Every time he kissed me, he did so with a deliberation that left me breathless. His lips would brush against mine, soft and lingering, as if he were memorizing every inch. He'd pull back just enough to let his breath hover over my skin, making my heart race, before diving back in, his kiss deeper, more insistent. His touch was confident yet tender, a blend of gentleness and passion that felt like he was completely wrapped up in me.

"You know I can't get enough of you," he'd murmur, his voice low. His hands would travel down my spine, fingers tracing a line that sent shivers along my skin as he pulled me closer, pressing his body against mine.

"Is that so?" I'd whisper, my voice barely audible, my pulse thrumming under his touch.

He'd smile then, a slow, teasing grin that told me he knew exactly what he was doing. He loved the effect he had on me, loved knowing that he held me there, lost and wanting, with every move. His hand would find my chin, tilting my face up to meet his gaze, and I'd find myself held captive by the depth in his eyes, his dark gaze full of both desire and something softer, something that felt achingly intimate.

"God, you're beautiful," he'd say, his voice filled with a quiet awe, almost as if he couldn't believe it himself. He'd press his forehead against mine, his hand tangled in my hair, and his lips would find mine again, slow and deliberate, igniting a fire within me that left me feeling vulnerable, open, and completely his.

As his hands moved down my shoulders, over my arms, he'd pull me even closer, the warmth of his body wrapping around me, anchoring me in a way that felt grounding. I could feel the steady rise and fall of his chest, the quiet rhythm of his breathing, and it was like we were moving together in perfect sync. He leaned over me, his face inches from mine, and I caught the glint of his chain above me, cool against the warmth between us. It was a reminder of how completely he had drawn me in, grounding me in the moment.

I reached up, fingertips grazing the cool metal before my hand settled against his neck, feeling the heat of his skin beneath. He watched me, his eyes full of something unspoken, a mixture of both desire and tenderness that left me breathless. The way he looked down at me, his gaze locked onto mine—it was as if he was branding this moment into my memory, as if he wanted me to remember every detail, every heartbeat.

"Do you have any idea what you do to me?" he'd whisper, his voice thick and barely controlled, his breath hot against my skin as his lips grazed my neck, igniting a spark that left me feeling completely unsteady.

"Tell me," I'd challenge, my voice shaky, a thrill coursing through me as he continued his slow, deliberate path along my skin. He'd just look at me, eyes dark with something raw and intense, as if he were caught between control and surrender. "You drive me insane," he'd say, his voice rough, filled with an unspoken need that sent a jolt through me. "I don't ever want this to end."

THE LAST 3 YEARS

And with those words, he'd lower his head, his hands pulling me closer, and I felt myself melting into him, feeling his heartbeat against mine, steady and grounding, as if I belonged here, with him, in this moment.

For a little while, all my doubts, all my fears faded away. All that mattered was the way he held me, the way he looked at me, the way he whispered my name like a secret only we shared. And as he kissed me, I felt like this—this pull, this passion, this intimacy—was all I would ever need.

*Chapter*

*8*

# The Weight of Promises

## *Initial Doubts*

Hope was one of those friends who always seemed to linger at the edges, popping up at every gathering and slipping into conversations as if she'd always been there. When Austin first introduced me to his friend group, Hope hadn't struck me as anything special. She was just another friend in the crowd, someone with a boyfriend of her own, someone I didn't see as a threat. I'd never been the jealous type, and I trusted Austin, maybe more than I trusted anyone. I had no reason to worry.

But over time, Hope became a presence I couldn't ignore. At every bonfire and every party, she was there, always the first to greet him, her arms around him in a hug that lasted a little too long. She had this way of leaning in, whispering to him with that little whiny voice that set my teeth on edge, always laughing just a bit too hard at his jokes. I'd see the way her hand would linger on his arm, the way she'd rest her head on his shoulder, the way her eyes would drift to him as if he was the only one in the room. It was subtle at first, little things I could brush off, but the more I noticed it, the harder it became to ignore.

Austin brushed it off every time I brought it up. "She's just like that," he'd say, almost annoyed that I even cared. "She has a boyfriend, remember? She's not into me." And for a while, I tried to believe him. I told myself I was just overthinking it, that I was letting my imagination get the better of me.

But then I started noticing things on social media. His comments on her posts, telling her how great she was, uplifting messages that didn't seem to fit the dynamic of a purely platonic friendship. Far better messages than what he would send me to brighten my day. And whenever we'd go out, like to bonfires with his friends, she'd somehow dodge me entirely, going straight to him like I wasn't even there. Even his friends noticed, mentioning how strange it was that she'd act that way around him. And every time I brought it up, Austin shrugged it off, unwilling to even have a conversation with her about it, almost as if he craved the attention from her.

I didn't ask him to block her—I didn't want to be that kind of girlfriend. I just wanted him to see things from my perspective, to understand why it bothered me. But he never did. He just told me he didn't want "drama" in his friend group, as if my feelings were something he could easily set aside. Eventually, he decided he had enough of my "nagging," and he blocked her, and for a while, I thought it was over. We didn't see her much after that, and when we did, we kept our distance. I thought we'd moved on, that maybe he finally understood.

### *The Breaking Point*

Then, one day, everything came crashing down. I found messages from her on his phone, hidden in Snapchat, from a brief break we'd taken months back when things had been tense between us. My heart sank as I scrolled through the messages, each one hitting harder than the last. His words, her words—together, they painted a picture of me as nothing more than an inconvenience.

They mocked me, insulted me, called me immature, and claimed he deserves someone better. The cruelest blow came when she went so far as to say she was repulsed by the thought of me being his girlfriend. It felt like a brutal confirmation of every insecurity I had tried to suppress.

And then there was the part that cut the deepest—the jokes about Hope and him taking me to the Grand Canyon, about Hope pushing me off and him sitting back to watch.

That's when I finally confronted him, feeling a wave of anger and hurt that I could barely contain.

I looked down at my hands, feeling the weight of everything I'd just read. The words "Grand Canyon" and "self-defense" echoed in my mind like a cruel joke. I couldn't hold it in any longer. He came down the stairs from his shower, and when I finally spoke, my voice shook.

"Do you even realize what you said?" I asked, looking him dead in the eyes.

"What're you trying to start now, Lily?" He snapped.

My blood boiled as I shoved the messages in his face. He barely glanced at the phone.

"You joked about pushing me off a cliff, Austin. You were laughing with her, telling her to keep talking, planning this whole ridiculous thing."

Austin shifted uncomfortably, avoiding my gaze. "I didn't mean it like that," he mumbled. "It was just a joke, and she's... you know how Hope is. She says stuff like that, and I didn't think it would hurt you because—"

"Didn't think it would hurt me?" I interrupted, my voice rising. "You know how uncomfortable I've been around her, how she treats me like I'm some placeholder. And you just sat there, cheering her on, acting like she was right."

He sighed and reached for my hand, which I pulled back. "Look, she doesn't mean any of it," he said, trying to stay calm. "She's just... she's just one of my friends. It's not like I wanted to hurt you."

"That's what you always say, Austin," I replied, my voice barely above a whisper. "You always say it wasn't meant to hurt me. But it does, every time. And you know it does, but you keep doing it." I swallowed hard, trying to hold back tears. "If you loved me, shouldn't that mean something? Shouldn't it mean putting me first, making me feel valued?"

I paced his room, rubbing my eyes, trying to find the point where everything went wrong.

He looked away, running a hand through his hair. "It's not that simple," he muttered. "Hope's a part of my life. I can't just cut her off."

"So where does that leave me?" I asked. "Am I supposed to just stand by, watching you tell her I'm not good enough for you? Letting her suggest other women you should be with, like I'm just a phase you'll grow out of?"

"I'll talk to her," he said, his tone almost dismissive. "If it really bothers you that much… I'll tell her to back off."

"Will you?" I asked, my voice laced with doubt. "Because every time you bring it up, you brush me off. You say you don't want drama, that you don't want to 'create issues' in your friend group. But that doesn't stop you from creating them between us, does it?"

He looked up at me, desperation flickering in his eyes. "I don't want to lose you, okay?" he said, his voice cracking. "I'm sorry. I didn't mean any of it. You're who I want, Lily. I have no interest in her. We've been friends for a long time; if we wanted to be together, we would've by now. I'll block her right now, I'll change, I promise. I just… I can't lose you, Lil. You're my person."

I let out a shaky breath, knowing that I'd heard those words before. But there was a part of me that wanted to believe him, to hold onto this small glimmer of faith that he might actually follow through this time.

"Fine," I said finally, crossing my arms as I looked away. "But if you care about me—really care about me—then prove it. I don't want to be just another option. I want to be a priority for you."

He nodded, reaching out to pull me close, and reluctantly, I let him. Deep down, I wondered how many times I would forgive him, how many promises he'd break before I finally let go. But for now, I held on, convincing myself that things would be different this time.

### What If

By the time we reached the later stages of our relationship, I never felt comfortable leaving Austin alone for a weekend. The trust we once had—or at least, the trust I thought we had—had been chipped away so many times that I couldn't shake the fear of what he might do when I wasn't there.

When Lina and William had their combined bachelor and bachelorette weekend, I should have been excited. It was a celebration for my cousin and her fiancé, a weekend to relax, have fun, and be surrounded by people I loved. And I did try to enjoy myself. I told myself that this was a chance to focus on me, to let go of the constant worry and just live in the moment.

And for a while, I did. I ended up having so much fun, laughing and bonding with my cousins and the rest of the bridal party. It felt good to step away from everything and just exist without the weight of Austin on my shoulders. But as the night wore on and I knew he was heading to Jacob and Amber's bonfire, the anxiety crept back in. I tried to push it aside, but my thoughts wouldn't let me.

*What if she's there?* The question looped in my mind, over and over. I tried to reason with myself, telling myself it didn't matter. *Well, if he does something, I'm sure he'll just be more affectionate toward me later. It'll be the same cycle over and over again.*

That thought stopped me in my tracks. I hated that I could predict his patterns so clearly. He'd lie, I'd find out, we'd fight, and then he'd try to make it up to me with sweet words and gestures that never lasted. It was a cycle I knew all too well, and yet I still clung to the hope that maybe this time would be different.

After the weekend was over, I found out that Hope had been at the bonfire the entire time. I don't even remember how I found out, but when I asked Austin about it, he told me she wasn't there. He lied straight to my face, as if I hadn't seen this same act play out before. And just like every other time, I was left questioning myself, wondering if I could trust what I knew to be true or if I was just imagining things.

So many moments like this left me questioning who I was. I wasn't just worried about what he might do; I worried about what it said about me. Was I weak for staying? Was I naive for believing he could change? Or was I just fooling myself, holding onto something that was already gone?

The truth is, I was scared. Scared of losing him, yes, but also scared of losing the version of myself that had been wrapped up in him for so long. Because if I let him go—if I walked away and stopped trying to hold it all together—who would I even be without him?

*Thursday, November 2, 2023*

*Sometimes, I wonder how many times I have to replay all of this in my mind before it stops hurting. Even now, months later, I still feel the sting from those moments, as if they're happening all over again. It's strange, to think of the little gut feelings I keep ignoring, all the moments I brush off just to keep the peace. I often wonder if those gut feelings I ignored were actually fragments of the truth—clues to things he was doing behind my back that I still don't fully know about. With Kayla and Hope, there are always signs, that sinking feeling in my stomach telling me something isn't right. But I convince myself, time after time, that I'm just being paranoid. That love means giving him the benefit of the doubt.*

*Kayla is supposed to be "just a friend," someone from school that he grew up with, nothing more. And yet, she's the one who shows me just how quickly he can betray me. I try to forgive him, try to believe he made a mistake, that he can change. But I know now that it's not a one-time thing. It's part of his pattern. He's done it before, who's to say he won't do it again?*

*And then there's Hope. She's supposed to be part of his circle, someone with her own life, her own relationship. But that doesn't stop her from stepping in, from pushing boundaries I thought he would respect. It's humiliating, watching someone I trust care so little about hurting me, both of them twisting my trust into something unrecognizable. They both make me feel so small, like I'm not worth protecting or respecting. And he lets it happen, again and again.*

*I catch myself wondering if I did something wrong, if there's something about me that isn't enough. Maybe if I were different, stronger, if I fought harder for my place in his life, things would be different. But deep down, I know that's just a lie I tell myself to make sense of the pain. It's not me. It's him—the way he can't commit, can't value what he has, and the way he lets others chip away at the love we've built.*

*It's just... sad. It's sad that I waste so much love on someone who doesn't even see it, sad that I trust people who only take advantage of it. I'm trying to move forward, to put this behind me with the hope that things will get better for us. But some days, it still feels like I'm standing in the middle of the mess he made, wondering if I'll ever feel whole again.*

*Chapter*

*9*

# Daisy

I've wanted a dog for as long as I can remember. From the time I was a little girl, I'd beg my parents for one, endlessly promising that I would take care of it, walk it, and feed it. But their answer was always the same: it was a big responsibility, and they didn't feel I was ready. Year after year, my dream of having a dog stayed just that—a dream.

That all changed on my 19th birthday, two months after Austin and I had started dating. It was the height of the Covid pandemic, and I was home from school. My parents decided it was the perfect time for me to be home with a dog, finally fulfilling a wish I'd carried in my heart for so long. I couldn't believe it—I was getting a dog.

I spent hours researching breeds, looking for reputable breeders, and making sure I was prepared to take on the responsibility I had always promised I was ready for. The next day, everything came together. Sophie came with me to meet the litter of puppies. I could hardly contain my excitement on the drive over, my heart racing at the thought of finally meeting the one who would change my life forever.

The moment we stepped into the room, a small puppy with a wagging tail ran right up to me and jumped up as if she already knew I was hers. I picked her up, and she nestled into my arms, falling asleep within minutes. I held her for an hour, completely in awe of her. I didn't need to see any other puppies—I knew she was the one.

I named her Daisy.

Over the next few days, my family and I prepared for her to come home. We bought her toys, a bed, food, and everything she could possibly need. I couldn't stop talking about her to anyone who would listen, including Austin. I expected him to share in my excitement—after all, he had dogs of his own and always talked about how much he loved them. But his reaction caught me off guard.

"I don't know, babe," he said hesitantly when I told him. "This is going to take up all your time. She's going to be your number one priority now."

His words stung. I tried to explain how much this meant to me, how I'd dreamed of this moment for years.

"Daisy isn't just a puppy," I said, trying to make him understand. "She's part of my future—our future. If we're building a life together, she'll be part of it. She's not going anywhere."

He didn't say much after that, but I could tell he wasn't thrilled. Looking back, I should've recognized it as a red flag. If he genuinely cared about me, he would have shared in my happiness instead of worrying about how it might inconvenience him. But at the time, I brushed it aside, thinking he just needed time to adjust.

When Daisy finally came home, my life changed in ways I couldn't have imagined. She was my constant companion, shadow, and source of unconditional love. It took a while for Austin to fully accept her as part of our life, but eventually, he warmed up.

Most weekends, Daisy came with me to Austin's house, where she loved playing with his dogs. His parents adored her, treating her like she was their grandchild. "There's our little Daisy girl!" his mom would say, her face lighting up whenever we arrived.

They always made me feel welcome, and Daisy quickly became part of the family. It was one of the few things about our relationship that felt truly effortless—Daisy brought joy to everyone she met.

Daisy was more than just a dog to me. She was my comfort and my lifeline during some of the hardest moments in my life. On bad days, she was there to nuzzle me, her big brown eyes filled with understanding.

On long drives to clear my head, she sat in the passenger seat, her head resting on my lap as if to say, I'm here.

And when Austin and I broke up, Daisy was there, too. She didn't need to say anything; her presence was enough. I remember sitting on the floor of my room, tears streaming down my face as she curled up beside me, her quiet comfort soothing a pain I thought would never end.

Daisy has been with me through it all—the good, the bad, and everything in between. She's more than a pet; she's my greatest gift, a dream come true, and a reminder that unconditional love exists, even when it's hard to find in people.

As I write this, she's lying next to me, her snoring filling the room. I can't imagine my life without her, and I'm endlessly grateful that she chose me that day.

*Chapter*

# 10

# Perfectly Planned, Painfully Missed

It was our two-year anniversary–February 7, 2022. Since our anniversary and Valentine's Day were so close, we decided to split the planning. I would organize our anniversary, and he'd take charge of Valentine's Day. Both weekends, we'd be at his house, and I was excited to create something memorable.

For our anniversary, I followed my tradition, crafting a scrapbook filled with photos and memories, with descriptions of everything we'd done each month. It was a lot of work, starting back in October, to have it ready, but I loved the thought of capturing our journey in those pages. I made reservations at a restaurant we'd never been to, right along the beach, with a view of the Delaware Bay glistening in the background. Dinner was fancy, something special just for us, and I covered the cost.

When we returned to his house, I had more surprises waiting. I'd made a cake with "2 Years" written on it and gathered gifts that overflowed from bags and boxes. In his room, I laid out a cozy blanket, arranged fake candles and rose petals, and played soft country music in the background. I asked him to wait upstairs as I put everything together. When he came down, his eyes fell on the scrapbook from our first year, alongside the new one for this year. We sat together, flipping through the pages, laughing and reliving our memories. It was one of my favorite nights with him, a night I'd poured my heart into because he'd meant so much to me.

But then came the following weekend–Valentine's Day. He'd made plans this time, but I quickly noticed a difference. He took me to a restaurant in Ocean City, one he'd once taken another girl to before we dated. It felt odd and impersonal, but I brushed it off, hoping the night would still be special. But at dinner, we hardly talked. He seemed distracted, more interested in the couple seated next to us than in our time together. Since I was still twenty, I couldn't drink, but he had enough for both of us and by the end of the night, he was too drunk to drive. So I found myself behind the wheel, with a long hour drive back to his house.

He mentioned he had "one more surprise," and turned on the GPS. We arrived at a small beachside ice cream parlor–closed, of course, in the dead of winter. I tried to laugh it off, but frustration was creeping in, and he just shrugged, saying, "Guess we'll just go home then." Disappointed, I drove us back, hoping for something else when we got there, but he had nothing planned.

He barely even made it through the drive, falling asleep beside me, leaving me to sit with the disappointment, feeling more alone than ever. When we finally got back, he gave me a few gifts, ones I'd listed out for him because, without guidance, he apparently didn't know me well enough to surprise me with thoughtful gifts, something I tried so hard to do for him. No flowers, no card. Just dinner, a closed ice cream shop, and a few items off the list he asked me to give him, while I'd spent hours planning each detail of our anniversary night to surprise him. Every little disappointment, every letdown added up, leaving me with a familiar ache. Once again, he'd let me down.

### Saturday, February 18, 2023

*I don't know what I expected tonight, but I thought it would feel... different. I thought maybe, just this once, he'd put as much thought into this as I did. I spent so much time planning every detail of our anniversary. I poured so much of myself into that night, wanting it to be perfect. And I thought he'd understand how much these little things matter. How much it matters to be seen, to feel chosen.*

*But tonight, sitting at that dinner table, he barely looked at me. The whole time, it felt like he was somewhere else, barely even present. I don't know why, but he seemed more interested in the couple sitting beside us, more engaged in glancing around the room than being there with me. When he drank more than usual, I tried to smile, tried to laugh it off, but the silence was like this wall between us that I couldn't break.*

*I wanted him to surprise me, to have something special planned, something that would make me feel like I mattered. But after the dinner, he just pointed us to a closed ice cream shop and shrugged it off like it was nothing. He didn't even check if it was open...*

*And then, when he fell asleep on the way home, it felt like I was driving in the dark, not just on the road, but in the relationship, too. Like I was trying to find my way with no one beside me, just me navigating the silence. I don't know why it hurts so much, but it does. I keep telling myself not to take it personally, that maybe he just doesn't know how to show how he feels. But tonight, it feels like I'm alone in this, like I'm the only one fighting to keep us together.*

*We were supposed to be celebrating Valentine's Day, and here I am on his couch, sitting beside someone who's fallen asleep for the second time tonight, wondering if I'll ever be enough. I wanted so much to believe that he could be that person for me. But right now, all I feel is this emptiness, this ache that I'm carrying something he doesn't even see.*

*Maybe he'll never know what it took for me to give so much, to love him with everything I had. Maybe he'll never understand how much it hurt to sit here tonight, realizing that no matter what I do, I can't make him feel the same way.*

*Chapter*

*11*

# Summers Like This

The months leading up to our vacation felt like an endless build-up of excitement. The year before, Austin had come along on my family trip to Ocean City, Maryland, but this year, things were different. My parents were going away separately, which meant Austin and I could plan our own little getaway. I poured myself into planning every detail, relishing the thought of our first real trip alone together. Just him and me, no one else around to share our time.

Beyond all the dinners and lazy beach days we imagined, we had something else in common that made every plan feel special: our love for music. One of our favorite things to do together was going to concerts. Over the years, we'd seen so many artists perform live, each concert a different chapter in the story we were building together. We'd stand shoulder to shoulder, his arm wrapped around me as we sang our favorite songs, letting the energy of the crowd pull us closer. Those nights were magic, where we'd lose ourselves in the music, feeling the beat under our skin and knowing we were exactly where we wanted to be—with each other.

So when we planned our trip, we knew it wouldn't be complete without a playlist of our favorite songs, the ones that had become soundtracks to our nights together. Whether it was a song that reminded us of a concert or one we'd listened to during a late-night drive, music was a thread that tied all our memories together. As we set out for Bethany Beach, Delaware, we had that playlist ready, filling the car with melodies that felt like pieces of our journey.

We borrowed his parents' camper, which seemed perfect; it gave us the freedom to go where we wanted, stay out late, and not worry about the usual vacation expenses. The idea of cooking our own meals, sitting by a bonfire, and having late-night talks under the stars felt like exactly the kind of memories I wanted to make.

On the first day, after setting up the camper, we went grocery shopping together, picking out all the little things we wanted for the week. I'd planned most of the meals, determined to keep it low-key and meaningful. We only chose a couple of restaurants to visit, and I liked that—it made the moments we'd eat out feel like part of the adventure, without taking away from the coziness of cooking together at our own little campsite.

Throughout the week, we did everything we'd talked about and more. We spent a day at the beach, watching the waves and people around us, laughing at each other as we ran from the water, and relaxing in the sun with no rush to go anywhere. Another day, we toured a few nearby wineries and breweries, sampling drinks and exploring together, everything feeling like a new discovery. At night, we'd sit by the fire outside the camper, wrapped in blankets, sipping our favorite drinks, just talking about anything and everything.

One night outside in our hammock, as we looked up at the stars, he wrapped his arms around me, pulling me close. "This is the life, isn't it?" he murmured, a soft smile on his face.

"Yeah, it really is," I replied, resting my head on his shoulder, feeling the warmth of the fire and the quiet hum of contentment settling around us.

There was something about being away from everything—our families, our routines, all the noise—that made this time together feel like a world of our own. I think that's what made it so special, why I felt a deeper connection with him that week. It was the first time I'd ever gone away with a boyfriend, so every little moment felt meaningful. I wanted to hold onto all of it—the laughter, the simple meals we shared, the way he'd look at me with that familiar smile as if he was just as happy as I was.

When the week came to an end, neither of us wanted to go back. We packed up reluctantly, both knowing we had to return to real life but wishing we could stretch that little slice of summer just a bit longer. It was the kind of week that left me hopeful for more—more moments, more summers, more nights just like that. But looking back now, I realize that those fleeting days were like our favorite songs. They felt infinite, yet each had to end, even if we weren't ready to say goodbye.

*Chapter*

# 12

# **Silent Nights**

Our first Christmas together felt like magic, as firsts often do. We'd been dating for almost a year, and we were very much in love. That year, I was filled with excitement at the thought of blending our traditions. We decided we'd spend Christmas Eve with his family and Christmas Day with mine—a plan that became our yearly routine. I'd never spent a holiday in this way before, splitting time between two families, but it made me feel like we were creating something uniquely ours.

"We always get a real tree," Austin had explained that first Christmas as we bundled up to head to the farm with his parents. The experience was new to me; my family always had a fake tree. I remember standing in the cold, sipping hot chocolate his mom had packed in a thermos, while his dad held up trees and Austin debated with his mom over which was "the one." I loved every minute of it. Being included in their tradition made me feel like I truly belonged, like I was part of their family.

"What do you think, babe?" Austin had asked, holding up a tree. "It's perfect," I said, even though I would've said that about any tree he chose.

He grinned, clearly pleased, and kissed my forehead before we loaded it onto the car.

As the years went on, Christmas became predictable, yet uneven. I always went out of my way to make the holiday special—for him, his family, and mine. I'd spend weeks carefully choosing thoughtful gifts for his parents, his sister, Annie, and her boyfriend, Brent. When it came to my family, Austin didn't put in the same effort. Every year, I'd find myself helping him pick out gifts for my parents, Nick, and Sophie because he never had a clue what to get them.

Worse, I was the one paying for those gifts on top of the gifts I bought for everyone else. I tried to justify it by telling myself it was easier this way—after all, I already knew what they'd like. But deep down, it hurt. Christmas wasn't just about the gifts; it was about the thought behind them, and Austin's lack of effort made his presents feel hollow.

"What should I get your mom?" he'd ask one year while scrolling aimlessly on his phone.

"She loves candles and books. Maybe something like that?" I offered.

"Can you just grab something for me when you're out shopping?" he said casually.

And so, I did. I bought the gifts, wrapped them, and labeled them as being from him. On Christmas Day, he'd hand them to my parents with a smile while I stood there silently, knowing I'd done all the work.

Each year, I made him a list of things I'd like for Christmas, thinking it would make things easier for him. He'd always ask for it, saying he didn't want to get me something I didn't want. But he rarely got everything on the list, even though the items were simple. I never asked for anything extravagant, just little things that I loved or needed. Meanwhile, I went above and beyond for him. If he mentioned wanting something—even offhandedly—I made sure he had it. I loved seeing his face light up when he unwrapped something he didn't expect but really wanted.

Of course, I was thankful for the gifts he gave me. But they always lacked meaning. They didn't reflect his knowing me deeply or paying attention to what I loved.

"Didn't you like your gifts?" he'd ask, noticing my hesitation one year.

"I did," I said, forcing a smile. But in my heart, I knew I wanted more than just gifts—I wanted effort.

I've always loved art and looked for ways to incorporate creativity into our holidays. One of my favorite ideas was making Christmas ornaments together. I imagined us sitting at the table with glitter, paint, and ribbons, laughing as we made one ornament for my tree and one for his. But every year, it ended the same: me alone at the table, crafting two ornaments by myself while he sat on the couch watching TV. "I'm just not creative, babe," he'd say, shrugging when I asked him to join.

"That's not the point. It's about doing it together," I tried to explain. But he never seemed to understand.

One of my favorite traditions has always been looking at Christmas lights. Nothing fills me with the holiday spirit like bundling up, drinking hot chocolate, and taking in the sparkle and magic of the season. I begged Austin to go with me every year.

"It's too cold," he'd complain one year.

"We don't have to walk around. We can just drive," I offered. "I'd rather stay home."

No matter how much I tried to persuade him, it was always an uphill battle. The only time we ever went was the final Christmas we spent together, just a few months before the breakup.

I had planned everything perfectly: hot chocolate in to-go mugs, Christmas music on the car radio, and a route that included the best-decorated neighborhoods by my house. I thought he'd enjoy it since he didn't even have to get out of the car.

At first, things seemed fine. Austin sat beside me, sipping his hot chocolate as I pointed out my favorite displays. But soon, he started nodding off.

"Austin, wake up," I said, nudging him. "Huh? Yeah, I'm awake," he muttered, only to doze off again minutes later. By the third or fourth time, I gave up. I let him sleep while I drove around, tears streaming down my face. I wanted to share something special with him, something that brought me so much joy, and he couldn't even stay awake for it. I parked the car back at my house, turned off the engine, and sat in silence before waking him up to go inside.

Looking back, those Christmases taught me a lot about the imbalance in our relationship. I wanted to build traditions, create memories, and share experiences that mattered. But no matter how much I gave, I always felt like I was left wanting more—not things, but effort, partnership, and love that matched mine.

*Chapter*

# 13

# Carrying It All

I've always had a nurturing personality. Taking care of people came naturally to me—an instinct I wore as both a blessing and a curse. Early in our relationship, I didn't mind reminding Austin of things: appointments, birthdays, including my own, plans we made. It felt like a way to show my love, a way to make his life easier.

But as time went on, it became a constant drain, like carrying a heavy bag that he never offered to take off my shoulders. Every plan, every detail—if I didn't keep track of it, it felt like no one would. And instead of being grateful, he'd snap, telling me, "I don't need a mom. I already have one. I need a girlfriend." At first, I laughed it off, but after the tenth or twentieth time, the words cut like glass.

One of the many ways I tried to support him was with his obsession: cars and trucks. In the early days, it was exciting, even endearing. I remember the time I surprised him with a test drive of his dream truck. His eyes lit up, and I thought, *This is worth it.* But over time, it became all-consuming. Every other conversation revolved around vehicles— what he wanted, what he couldn't afford, what he'd missed out on. His dreams of owning over 20 vehicles turned into a fixation, eclipsing date nights and even our relationship.

The dealership incident added to the growing mental load.

It was a Friday, and I was at my internship when he texted me a link to his dream truck—a sleek, low-mileage model just a short drive from his house.

"It's perfect," he wrote, followed by a string of exclamation points.

I smiled, hearing the excitement in his words, even through a text. "Want to go check it out after work?" I replied.

"Yeah, let's do it."

I was trying to be positive, but in the back of my mind, I could already feel the tension creeping in. By now, I knew how these truck-buying trips usually went. They started with excitement but often ended in disappointment—and sometimes, an argument.

Before we left his house, I asked him, "Do you have everything you need? A recent statement for your current truck payment? Anything they'll ask for?"

He sighed loudly, his shoulders slumping. "Why do you always do this?"

"Do what?" I asked, genuinely confused.

"Act like my mom. Stop being a mother. You're my girlfriend. I already have a mom," he said, rolling his eyes.

I bit my tongue. I didn't want to start a fight before we even left. "I'm just trying to help," I said softly.

At the dealership, things started off smoothly. The test drive went well, and for a moment, I let myself hope that maybe this time would be different. But as soon as we sat down with the salesman, the cracks began to show. Austin struggled to log in to his app to retrieve his truck payment details.

"Did you bring the login info with you?" I asked cautiously.

"I thought I had it," he muttered, staring at his phone. His tone was already clipped.

"Maybe you could check your email?" I suggested. "I'm not an idiot. I've already checked," he snapped.

I flinched but kept my voice steady. "Okay, do you want me to look through the papers you brought? Maybe it's in there."

"Why?" he barked, glaring at me.

"To help you," I said, my voice trembling with restrained frustration.

He shoved the papers across the table, his movements sharp and dismissive. The salesman stood awkwardly, excusing himself to give Austin more time to gather his information. I flipped through the documents, but of course, there was nothing useful in the stack.

"Maybe your mom would know the login information?" I offered. "Do you want me to text her?"

He whipped his head up from his phone, his face twisted in irritation. "Leave me alone. You're not helping by nagging me."

The words hit me like a slap. I felt the heat rise in my chest, the anger bubbling to the surface. Without a word, I stood abruptly, the chair scraping loudly against the floor, and stormed away from the table. I walked quickly to the bathroom, my hands shaking as I locked the door behind me. I leaned against the sink, my breath shallow and rapid, tears stinging my eyes.

When I returned from the bathroom, I saw Austin sitting across from the salesman, his posture relaxed, his face composed. The frustration he had directed at me earlier seemed to have completely evaporated. He nodded politely as the salesman went over the numbers, calmly listening to the breakdown of the costs.

When the bad news finally came—that the monthly payment was far out of his budget—Austin didn't flinch. Instead, he extended his hand, a polite smile on his face. "Thank you for your time," he said, his tone measured and courteous. "I really appreciate you working with me."

I stood there in silence, stunned. Where was this version of him when he spoke to me? The patience, the understanding, the respect—it was all reserved for the salesman, a stranger. I couldn't help but compare his kind words and pleasant demeanor to the sharp, dismissive tone he had used with me just minutes earlier. My chest tightened as I replayed his earlier words: *You're not helping. Stop nagging me.*

He had spoken to me as if I were a disturbance, an obstacle in his way. But with the salesman, he was poised and gracious, thanking him profusely for his time even though the outcome wasn't what he had hoped for. It was infuriating, the way he could so easily offer respect to a stranger while dismissing the person who had spent years supporting him.

As he started the car, I couldn't contain my thoughts any longer. "It's amazing," I began, my voice trembling, "how polite you can be to someone you've known for twenty minutes but not to me."

He glanced at me, confused. "What are you talking about?"

"You thanked him," I said, my tone sharper now. "You shook his hand, smiled, and spoke to him like he mattered. Meanwhile, you treated me like I was a problem. Like I didn't matter at all."

His face hardened, and he gripped the steering wheel tightly. "I was frustrated," he muttered. "I didn't mean to take it out on you."

"Frustrated?" I repeated, my voice rising. "Frustrated doesn't give you the right to speak to me like that. You don't see it, do you? How disrespectful you were? How embarrassed you made me feel?"

He sighed heavily, as if my words were an inconvenience. "I said I'm sorry, okay? What more do you want?"

I stared out the window, swallowing the lump in my throat. What more did I want? Respect, understanding, love—all the things he seemed capable of giving so freely to others, but never to me when I needed them most.

The rest of the ride was silent, but the tension hung heavy in the air. Back at his house, I tried to push my emotions aside as we discussed how we were going to try to find the balance on his truck, so he could possibly get a better offer.. I suggested calling my brother Nick for advice, and Austin reluctantly agreed.

As I explained the situation to Nick over the phone, Austin's mood darkened again. When I mentioned his current truck payment, he stormed upstairs without a word.

After I hung up, he came back down, his face flushed with anger. "Why would you tell your brother about my payment?" he demanded.

"It's not a secret, Austin," I said, my voice weary. "He's trying to help."

"It's my business," he snapped. "You tell your family too much about me."

The argument escalated quickly, his words cutting deeper with every exchange. Finally, I couldn't take it anymore. I stormed out of the house, tears blurring my vision as I drove aimlessly. His calls came one after another, but I ignored them, trying to calm the storm inside me.

When I finally answered, his voice was softer, almost pleading. "Please come back," he said. "I'm sorry for snapping. I didn't mean to hurt you. I just... I get stressed, and I take it out on you. It's not fair, and I know that."

His apology was enough to bring me back, but the weight of care I carried for him lingered, heavier than ever.

*Chapter*

# 14

# You Look So Good in Love

I know what you might be thinking: *Lily, why the hell did you choose to stay for so long? Or, what made him so special to stay?* Trust me, I've asked myself those same questions more times than I can count. And yet, when I look back, the answers are complicated. It wasn't just one thing; it was a mix of small, beautiful moments that kept me holding on, even when I knew deep down that the foundation of our relationship was cracking.

In the beginning, Austin had a way of making me feel special in ways that caught me completely off guard. Like the time he surprised me with a Swarovski koala crystal because he knew it was my favorite animal. I hadn't even mentioned my love for them often, but he remembered. When he handed it to me, his shy smile tugging at the corner of his lips, I felt a warmth I hadn't known before.

"I saw it and thought of you," he said, rubbing the back of his neck like he was nervous. "It's dumb, right?"

"It's not dumb at all," I replied, holding it tightly in my hands. "It's perfect. Thank you."

His face lit up at my response, and in that moment, I felt like he truly saw me. It was such a thoughtful gesture, the kind that made me believe he genuinely cared.

Then there was a pre-Valentine's Day surprise, our third one we would be spending together. I had gone out earlier that day to get my nails done with Kate, excited to spend the evening with Austin, having no idea what he had planned. When I got back to his house, I opened the door and saw a trail of rose petals starting at the top of the stairs.

"Austin?" I called out, confused but intrigued.

"Just follow the petals," he replied from somewhere downstairs, his voice laced with a playful tone.

My heart skipped a beat as I followed them, step by step, down to the foot of his bed. There, he had made a sign that read, *Will you be my Valentine?* Next to it was a beautiful bouquet of flowers and a bottle of wine. I stood there, stunned and overwhelmed with emotion.

"You did this for me?" I asked, turning to him as he stepped into the room.

"Of course I did," he said, grinning. "You deserve it."

I threw my arms around him, my smile so wide it hurt. "This is amazing, Austin. I thought you said you didn't need to ask me to be your valentine since I was already your girlfriend."

"Yeah, I know," he admitted, laughing. "But I wanted to."

It was sweet and meaningful—something I didn't have to ask for. He had taken the time to make the day special for me, and in that moment, it felt like he truly saw me, like he wanted to make me happy.

And then there were moments like the night we went to the beach. It was the middle of winter, bitterly cold, and close to midnight, when Austin asked if I wanted to get out of the house for a while.

"Do you want to do something crazy?" he asked, his eyes glinting with excitement.

I raised an eyebrow. "What kind of crazy?"

"Not illegal crazy," he said, laughing. "Just... spontaneous. There's this spot I want to take you to. Trust me."

We picked up a pizza on the way to this quaint, quiet beach near his house. The world was still, the kind of silence that only comes with winter nights. We sat in the bed of his truck, the waves crashing softly in the background as we ate our pizza under a blanket and a sky full of stars.

"I love it here," I said, leaning back and gazing up at the sky. "It's so peaceful."

"I thought you would," he replied, brushing crumbs off his hands. He leaned back, "Sometimes I come here when I need to clear my head."

We didn't talk much that night. We didn't need to. His phone played country music—songs we both loved, songs that felt like they were written for moments like this.

"You're not cold?" he asked, noticing me shiver slightly.

"A little," I admitted, laughing. "But it's worth it."

He draped his jacket over my shoulders without a word, as he wrapped his arm around me and pulled me closer. In those moments, there was nothing that could come between us. I felt safe, happy, and completely content, as if time had paused just for us. It was one of the few times I thought, *This is what love is supposed to feel like.*

But as time went on, those unexpected acts of love and those perfect nights became fewer and farther between. I found myself wishing we had done more things that brought us closer together, hoping that these moments could last forever. Instead, Austin often fell into patterns that made me feel disconnected. On our planned dates, he'd either fall asleep or drink to no end.

Before he reached the stage of being wasted, he was flirty and fun—less tense than usual. Those moments, brief as they were, reminded me of the Austin I fell for. He'd make jokes, pull me close, and laugh like nothing else mattered. I wished he could stay in that stage, where the drinks loosened him up just enough to let his guard down without letting everything spiral out of control. If only he could have stopped there, at that comfortable stage where we were just having fun.

But he couldn't. He didn't. He always pushed past that point, drinking to the point of not being able to function. Those moments of fun and connection disappeared as quickly as they came, leaving me to pick up the pieces. At first, the falling asleep didn't bother me—I understood. He worked long hours, got up early, and sometimes even worked Saturdays. Of course, he was tired.

Over time, his constant falling asleep became an annoyance. Every single movie we watched together, he fell asleep. The first and last time we ever went to the movies was during the last New Year's we spent together. He had been begging me for months to see this movie with him, and I finally gave in.

"You better stay awake this time," I teased as we walked into the theater.

"I will," he promised, laughing. "This is the one movie I've been dying to see."

I even paid for the tickets, thinking, *Maybe this time he'll stay awake.* But halfway through, I glanced over to see him slumped in his seat, head tilted back, snoring softly.

"Austin," I whispered, nudging him gently. "Wake up."

"Huh?" he muttered, sitting up and rubbing his eyes. "I wasn't asleep."

"Yes, you were," I said, trying to hold back my frustration. "Why did you even want to come if you were just going to sleep through it?"

"I'm tired, okay?" he snapped softly, slumping back in his seat.

I didn't push it, but the disappointment sat heavy in my chest. I had hoped, just this once, that he'd be present with me.

And once again, I sat in silence and watched the movie, one I didn't care much to see, while he slept his way through the whole thing.

Still, there were moments of joy that reminded me why I stayed. He was funny when you got to know him, with a dry, sarcastic humor that could make me laugh until my stomach hurt. He was also incredibly passionate, and I admired that about him. Whether it was about his goals, his hobbies, or the rare times he seemed truly happy in our relationship, his passion was undeniable.

When he was passionate about me, it felt intoxicating. Like the time he danced with me in the kitchen, spinning me around while a random playlist blared from his phone. Or the way he'd send me songs he loved that reminded him of me, his texts filled with excitement as he asked, *"Did you listen yet? What do you think?"*

In those moments, it felt like everything would be okay, that all the fights, hurt, and tears shouldn't break us because, in those moments, I saw what our future together could be like.

*Chapter*

# 15

# The Bottom of the Bottle

### *The Early Signs*

In the beginning, I didn't think much of Austin's drinking. Maybe I brushed it off as normal, something a lot of young guys did. But even early on, there were warning signs I missed–or maybe just chose to ignore. The first time I saw him really lose control was the first year we were together, at my cousin's wedding. It was supposed to be a celebration, a night to have fun and enjoy being surrounded by friends and family. But Austin was celebrating more than anyone else. By dinner, he was slurring his words, stumbling over himself, and barely able to hold his drink in his hand. At one point, he disappeared into the bathroom, and I got worried. I had to pull my brother aside, ask him to check on Austin, and make sure he was okay.

We left the reception, but the night didn't end there. In the parking lot, Austin started an argument, frustrated and defensive, twisting my words and accusing me of things I hadn't said. We argued for over half an hour, his anger rising in waves that I couldn't reason with. It was the first of many nights that left me feeling like a stranger to him, wondering who this version of Austin really was. My mom noticed, too.

She watched it all from a distance, disappointment plain on her face. From that night on, I could feel her disapproval, the tension every time she looked at us. She never really trusted him after that, and honestly, I couldn't blame her.

### Steady Pour of Disappointment

Over the next two years, I got used to it. I got so good at managing him when he was drunk that it became second nature. We'd go out to dinner, concerts, or family gatherings, and most of the time, he'd drink to the point where he couldn't drive home. I'd bring him back to my house or his, where he'd inevitably fall asleep in the car. I'd have to drag him inside, coaxing him toward the bathroom so he wouldn't wet the bed. Those were the nights when he'd twist my words, his frustration laced with an anger I didn't deserve. And those were the nights I felt the most alone.

It wasn't just parties or dinners with friends. Even at his mom's house, he'd drink to excess. There were nights Pam and I would be sitting upstairs, playing cards, while he polished off a case of beer on his own. She'd laugh, saying, "He's your problem now," like it was a joke, but I knew what that really meant. She knew I'd always be the one to get him to bed, to keep an eye on him, to make sure he didn't choke on his own vomit or suffocate himself by falling asleep on his face. Even when I finally turned 21, the drinking didn't ease up. In fact, it felt worse. Nights I wanted to let go a little, to finally enjoy myself, ended with me watching over him, sobering up fast enough to get us home. I was never free of that responsibility because he couldn't control himself.

### A Toast to Embarrassment

Lina and William's wedding in the summer of 2023 was supposed to be about love and family—a chance for everyone to come celebrate her new beginning. A weekend I was looking forward to being a part of since I was a bridesmaid, and Lina and I talked about this day since we were little. It was a beautiful weekend, starting with a small ceremony at the church on Friday. Afterward, we gathered in her parent's backyard, and I helped capture the day, taking photos that would become memories in the years to come. But as the sun set, and the day turned into an intimate celebration, Austin turned into another episode of his drinking. By dessert, he was the only one who thought jumping into the pool on my cousin's wedding day was a good idea. He didn't care about how it looked; it was just another thing to shrug off for him, but for me, it was a familiar pang of embarrassment.

The rest of the weekend was spent preparing for Lina's big wedding ceremony on Sunday at a nearby venue. I offered to help Lina and William, bringing decorations from their house to the hotel where everyone would be staying. Austin rode with me, along with Nick and Sophie, who came along to help. But Austin had been drinking since early in the day, and his mood was far from stable. As I drove, he grew paranoid and loud, suddenly convinced I had taken his phone. His words slurred, and his tone edged with aggression as he reached over, grabbing at my side, accusing me of stealing it, though I had nothing to do with it. Nick and Sophie sat in the backseat, silent and visibly uncomfortable, watching the scene unfold. I was humiliated, both for the situation he was creating and for the way he spoke to me in front of others.

Eventually, he fell asleep in the car, and for a moment, there was peace. But the discomfort lingered. Nick and Sophie's silence said more than words; I could feel their quiet judgment and concern, and it made me see how much I had normalized.

The drinking wasn't confined to weekends or special occasions, either. He drank nearly every day after work. By the time we'd get on the phone at night, he'd already be several drinks in, and I'd worry. I'd lie awake, listening to his breathing, praying he wouldn't throw up in his sleep. Sleep became elusive on those nights, my mind racing with scenarios I couldn't control.

### Spilling Over

But the night that finally broke me was his stepsister Annie's engagement party. It had been raining heavily, and I volunteered to drive us there in his stepdad's new truck. I was nervous–new truck, bad weather–but I managed. When we arrived, I wasn't worried about Austin drinking much; the options were limited. But somehow, he found a way. By the end of the party, he was more than tipsy, leaning on me as we left.

When Annie invited us to join them at a bar afterward, I was hesitant. I wasn't in the mood to go out, but Austin didn't ask what I wanted; he immediately agreed, leaving me with little choice. At the bar, Annie's fiance's best man threw his credit card on the table and told everyone to order what they wanted, and to Austin, it was an invitation to lose himself. I lost count of how much he drank. By the time we left, he was barely able to stand, swaying and stumbling with each step. I had to support him as we moved through the crowd.

He needed to use the bathroom, so I helped him to the men's room by the door and told everyone we'd meet them outside. Ten or fifteen minutes passed, and he still hadn't come out. I knocked on the door, and a few seconds later, he swung it open, standing there in the doorway with his pants to his knees, completely oblivious. My stomach dropped as I realized everyone in the bar was watching, staring at us. Humiliated and furious, I grabbed him by the collar, and with my teeth clenched, I said, "Get your fucking shit together." I pushed him back into the bathroom and slammed the door, my whole body shaking. He stumbled out a few minutes later with no memory of what had just happened.

The next morning, he was a wreck, throwing up all day. I swore he had alcohol poisoning, but he brushed it off as a bad hangover. When I finally left to go home, I looked at him and said, in front of his mom, "I'm not putting up with this much longer." His mom didn't say a word. I think, in some way, she knew it too. The drinking, the recklessness, the fights–it had all piled up into something too heavy for me to carry alone. And as I walked out that day, I knew that the end was closer than either of them realized.

In those last two weeks with Austin, it felt like a storm brewing within me, tearing apart every ounce of certainty I once held. I kept replaying every lie, every broken promise, each moment that exposed cracks in the image of us I'd tried so hard to protect. It was as if my mind was unraveling from within, tangled in a relentless mix of confusion, sadness, and pain. For so long, I had kept everything between us to myself—shielding him from judgment, maybe even preserving the version of our relationship I desperately wanted to believe in. But as the weight became unbearable, I finally let others in.

### *Friday, May 10, 2024*

*I still remember that night at Annie's engagement party, not just for how out of control Austin was but for something else that lodged itself in my memory. We were all sitting together at the bar—Austin, Annie, her fiancé Brent, and their friends. And then there was Cassie, Annie's maid of honor. It was funny how quickly Cassie and I fell into a conversation, chatting about school and future plans, and somehow, even astrology came up.*

*Cassie and I weren't close, but we'd seen each other enough over the years. She'd even invited Austin and I to her wedding—the first wedding we ever went to together. She was genuinely interested in what I was studying and what career path I wanted to take. But then, as she asked Austin to join in, her excitement shifted to something else, something more cautious.*

*He was so drunk, he could barely put words together. She tried to ask about our anniversary plans, a simple question, but he was stumbling over his sentences, swapping words around, not even making sense. I wanted to shrink in my seat, embarrassed and drained. I watched her eyes shift back to me, a moment of understanding in her gaze, like she could see through the haze of everything I had tried to brush off about Austin.*

*Then she leaned in, her voice low as she said something I would never forget: "You're a Taurus? And Austin too, but in May?" She raised her eyebrows, leaning even closer and whispering, "Men born in May that are Tauruses… they're the strangest men. They're unloyal, confusing, and can be narcissistic." She told me about someone she once dated who had the same sign as Austin, the strange and unsettling traits he had, almost as if she was describing Austin himself. Her words sent a jolt through me; I wasn't into astrology, but at that moment, I wondered if she was onto something—if maybe she saw something I was ignoring or couldn't admit to myself.*

*That night, I kept replaying her words in my head, even as I helped Austin stumble his way out of the bar. Something about the way she looked at me, the quiet understanding in her voice, stayed with me long after that night. It was like she saw through the layers of loyalty and hope I'd wrapped myself in, straight to the doubts I kept buried.*

*I wonder if Cassie saw something in him that I couldn't bring myself to see. Or maybe she saw it in me—the silent worry, the cracks in the image of us I was trying so hard to hold together. I still don't know if astrology has anything to do with it, but I do know one thing: that night, she planted a seed of truth that only grew over time, the kind that doesn't leave, even when you wish it would.*

*Chapter*

# 16

# The Final Fracture

**Friday, January 19, 2024**

I stayed home today. I usually go to Austin's on Fridays and stay till Sundays. Austin and I are apart, and I'm not entirely sure how I feel about that right now. We have spent every weekend together for the past three years. Sometimes, not the whole weekend, but on a regular weekend, we see each other Fridays, Saturdays, and Sundays.

We're in a weird place right now. He hasn't been the same with me lately, but I also feel like he hasn't changed. I'm changing, and I feel it. I can't ignore it anymore. Something is missing. Of course, I still love him and always will, but I'm just worried about the future. Will he change? Will he continue to do what he's doing forever? Can I live with that? It's a lot of emotions, but I know there's a good chance things won't change.

I always seem to be the one fixing all of our problems. He will never see an issue with things unless I bring them up. It often makes me question why he does this. Doesn't he know me well enough to see how I'm sad or upset about something? I've become very bitter. I'm not as happy as I used to be. I'm constantly worried about what he's doing on his phone and what's with him clicking on all these girls' social media profiles??

*He tells me that he loves me, but I need reassurance, and that is not reassuring me that he loves me. He doesn't realize it, but he's slowly losing me. I used to get so happy when we saw each other, when we would FaceTime, when we texted. Now, I have zero emotion. It's hard to admit all of this, but at the end of the day, how can I keep going and feel like this? I want to be in a relationship with him, but he's not willing to commit to a permanent change. What's left to do?*

*I do everything I can to do my part in this relationship. I used to do a lot more, but when you don't get the same effort and love in return, you slowly give up. No more long good morning texts, no more letters, no random gifts, no surprises, less up his ass. Everything just seems to piss him off. Everything I did just seemed to go unnoticed.*

*I don't get random cute "I'm thinking of you" texts—just silence most of the time. Don't get me wrong; I get that he's busy at work, but not for nothing. If you can scroll on social media to check out other girls and pay money for only fans while you're working, you could text me back. And, of course, when I confront him about it, he says he'll do better; he never meant to hurt me. He makes all of these promises that he only keeps for a couple of weeks, and then it's back to the same old Austin. Sometimes, I want him to hurt me just so I can feel what it's like for him to show me some above-average affection, even if it's for only a short while.*

*I do need to work on myself. No one's perfect, but my god, is it so hard for him to put me first sometimes? He's always on his phone, and god forbid, if I try to talk to him, it's like I'm interrupting his whole life. The only time we're close is when we're sleeping together and when I ask for a hug, which, by the way, he makes me feel like the largest piece of trash when he hugs me. Always trying to push me off, constantly complaining that he had enough. I wish he would love me as much as he loved eBay, whiskey, watches, and cars. He's so focused on everything else that he leaves me falling through the cracks. He takes me for granted a lot.*

*Our FaceTimes aren't as genuine anymore; we talk about our days, and then we're off doing our own thing. I just wish things were better. I want to feel like the person he wants for the rest of his life, not like his roommate. Still, after three years, he hasn't planned or taken me on any dates without me having to ask, maybe two times in our relationship? I just wish he would step up because, honestly, I don't know how much longer I can keep feeling like this.*

~ ~ ~

The last two weeks with Austin didn't just come out of nowhere. They were the result of a slow, relentless buildup of all the hurts and disappointments I'd pushed down over the three years we were together. Every broken promise, every lie, every betrayal—each one became a weight I'd tried to carry quietly, hoping that somehow he'd change. But as those final weeks approached, it was like I couldn't suppress it anymore; the cracks that had formed over time were breaking open, and I was left facing the truth I'd tried so hard to ignore.

About a week before things really began to unravel, Austin and I were spending an evening upstairs with his mom, Pam. She and I were playing a card game, one of those simple moments we'd both come to enjoy. Austin, though, was in a different world, sitting on his phone with his earbuds in, his mood distant and withdrawn. When I asked if he was okay, he got defensive, shutting down any attempt I made to reach him. I could feel it—that familiar sense that something was off. After all this time, I was a pro at reading him, and I knew that when he got into these moods, it usually meant he was hiding something.

Eventually, he left his phone downstairs to charge and went to shower before bed. As he walked away, I felt that gut instinct kick in—the one that had never failed me, the one that told me when there was something I needed to see. I reached across the room, opened his phone, and found what I'd suspected. In his search history were searches for Hope, Kayla, and even some of his ex-girlfriends he supposedly had blocked long ago. It was such a small act in comparison to the other hurts, but it felt like the final piece of proof that I couldn't ignore.

When he came back into the room, I didn't keep what I'd found to myself. Confronting him wasn't a choice anymore—it felt necessary, like I had to say something to release the pressure building inside me.

"What were you thinking?" I demanded, unable to hold back. "You just sat upstairs on that couch, two feet away from me, and thought, 'Well, now's the perfect time to look these girls up'? How delusional are you, Austin?"

He shifted uncomfortably, his face tight with anger. "I wasn't looking them up then," he muttered defensively. "I don't remember when it was, but I didn't do it in front of you."

My patience snapped. "The timestamps on the searches were from a half hour ago, Austin. We were *upstairs,* and your ass was on that couch, snapping at me, saying you were fine, that nothing was bothering you—all while doing this?"

I watched him as he tried to gather himself, his defensiveness turning into frustration. The betrayal wasn't just in his actions—it was in his ability to sit beside me, pretending everything was fine while he was actively betraying my trust. His face was a familiar mask of regret, but I couldn't bring myself to believe it anymore. His apologies had worn thin, each one blending into the next until they all felt hollow, rehearsed.

As the argument spiraled, he threw the same lines at me he'd used so many times before—how I was the one who couldn't trust him, how I was the one holding us back from moving forward. It was all so exhausting, a loop we'd been caught in for too long, the same empty promises, the same attempts to make me doubt my own instincts.

But this time was different. Our bed, the place where we'd shared so many moments of closeness and vulnerability, felt cold and unfamiliar. I no longer felt safe in the space that was supposed to be ours. Instead, it felt like a place of distance, a place where lies and betrayal had taken root. I went through the motions, forgiving him again, just as I'd done so many times before. But the forgiveness felt forced and hollow, and the weight of everything I'd been carrying wouldn't go away. It only grew stronger, gnawing at me, keeping me awake at night, filling me with unease every time I wasn't with him.

In those last days, I began to see our future for what it was—a cycle of betrayal, apologies, and broken promises. For the first time, the thought of leaving felt like a door opening, a glimpse of life without the constant hurt. And for once, the idea of life without him felt more like freedom than fear.

*Chapter*

# 17

# Falling Apart

One morning, instead of going to school, I couldn't ignore the weight pressing down on me. It felt like it had finally grown too heavy to carry on my own, and I knew I had to let it out. Without hesitation, I drove to Alyssa's apartment, hoping she'd know how to handle the tangled mess of my emotions, even though she'd never seen me like this.

When I walked in, she looked up from her coffee, her brow furrowing as she took in my tear-streaked face. "Lily? What's wrong?" she asked, standing up and crossing the room in seconds.

I shook my head, barely able to get the words out. "It's… everything. Austin, me, everything."

She guided me to the couch, her arm around my shoulders as I started to cry. "Okay," she said softly. "Take your time. Tell me what's going on."

I took a shaky breath and began to unload it all: every betrayal, every doubt, every broken part of myself I'd tried to hold together for so long. "He keeps lying to me, Alyssa," I said, my voice trembling. "And every time, I tell myself it'll get better. That he'll change. But he doesn't, and I feel like… like I'm disappearing trying to keep this relationship together."

She stayed quiet, her eyes softening with empathy as I poured everything out, not just the betrayals but the anger, the confusion, and the exhaustion. "I don't even know who I am anymore," I admitted, my hands twisting nervously in my lap. "I'm just so tired."

When I was done, Alyssa leaned forward, her expression gentle but firm. "Lily, you already know what you need to do, don't you?" she said, her voice steady but kind.

I stared at her, my heart pounding. "What do you mean?" "You know." she said softly. "Deep down, you've known for a long time. You're just scared to admit it."

Her words hit like a tidal wave, and for the first time, I couldn't fight the truth anymore. I nodded slowly, tears welling in my eyes again. "I don't want to lose him, Alyssa. But I don't know how to keep going like this."

She reached out and squeezed my hand. "You're not losing him, Lily. He's already lost you. You're just holding onto the version of him that doesn't exist anymore."

The release of opening up to Alyssa made it easier to reach out to Sophie. One afternoon, after what felt like an endless cry in my room, I knew I couldn't sit with the weight alone any longer. I sent her a text, and she immediately replied, telling me to meet her and Nick at the park.

When I arrived, Sophie hugged me tightly. "Okay, start from the beginning," she said, her tone calm but concerned.

As we walked slowly through the trees, I told them everything. I spoke about the lies, the constant cycle of hope and disappointment, and the way I felt like I was slowly losing myself. Sophie listened patiently, grounding me with her steady presence.

"You're so much stronger than you think," she said softly when I finished. "I believe in you, Lily. Whatever you decide, I'll be here. You're not doing this alone."

Nick's response was different. He had been quiet the entire time, his jaw tight as I talked. When I finally looked at him, unsure of what he was thinking, he said, "Lily, none of this is on you. He's the one who messed up. Not you."

"I feel like it's my fault," I admitted, my voice small. "Like if I had done something different—"

"Stop," he interrupted, his tone firm but not unkind. "This isn't your fault. Austin made those choices. And honestly? He doesn't deserve you."

His calm strength surprised me, but it also gave me something solid to lean on. I knew he hated seeing me this way, and he made it clear that he'd support whatever choice I made.

Lina's response hit differently. She'd known parts of the story and seen hints of my hurt, but hearing everything made her realize how deep the wounds went. When I finished, she looked at me with tears in her eyes. "Lily, why didn't you tell me sooner?"

"I didn't want to bother anyone," I said quietly, looking down. "And... I didn't want anyone to think less of him."

She reached over and pulled me into a hug. "You're my cousin. You're family. I don't care what he's done—I care about you.

I rested my head on her shoulder, feeling a weight lift just knowing she was there. "Thank you," I whispered.

"You don't have to thank me," she said firmly. "We all love you, Lily. We just want you to be happy."

Telling my parents was the hardest part. I hesitated for days, worried that if I ever decided to give things another chance, they'd never see him the same way again. But eventually, the pain became too much to keep inside. One night after dinner, I sat them down, my heart pounding.

"I need to tell you something," I began, my voice trembling. My mom immediately leaned forward, her face filled with concern. "It's about Austin."

As I told them everything, my mom's expression shifted from worry to concernment. When I finished, she reached over and took my hand. "Lily, you don't have to go through this alone," she said softly. "Whatever you decide, your dad and I will be here. We'll catch you if you fall. You just need to do what's best for you."

Her words brought tears to my eyes, and I leaned into her embrace. "I'm scared," I admitted. "I don't know if I'm strong enough."

"You are," she said firmly. "You're stronger than you realize. And you'll figure this out, one step at a time."

Hearing her say that gave me a sense of peace I hadn't felt in weeks. For the first time, I started to believe that maybe, just maybe, I could get through this.

## Unfinished Endings

In those last two weeks with Austin, it felt like an endless loop of endings that never quite ended. We broke up twice, both times leaving me feeling like I was caught between wanting to walk away and being terrified of what life would look like without him. I didn't know myself outside of him anymore.

The first breakup happened over FaceTime. We spent the entire call going in circles, Austin trying to understand what I wanted while I struggled to put my tangled feelings into words.

"I don't know what I want anymore," I admitted, my voice thick with emotion. "I feel so broken from everything, from all the hurt you've put me through, but I don't even know a life without you anymore."

He looked back at me through the screen, his face etched with confusion. "So what are you saying, Lil? You want to break up?"

I hesitated, searching his face for some sign of remorse, something that might tell me this could still be fixed. But I only saw the same desperation, the same cycle we'd been stuck in for years.

"I don't know, Austin," I whispered, feeling lost in my own words. "I just don't know."

We went back and forth, our voices growing louder, emotions swirling as we argued about everything and nothing at once. It was exhausting, draining every ounce of energy I had. Something about him still had a hold on me, and despite everything, we decided to keep trying. I hung up feeling even more confused than before, knowing we'd only put a temporary Band-Aid on something far deeper.

## False Hope

Then, a few days later, I suggested we go out to celebrate my internship offer—my senior placement, something I'd worked so hard for. I wanted to share this milestone with him, hoping it might bring us closer, even if just for a moment. He agreed, and we decided to go to a brewery he liked. We planned to meet after he was done with work and I finished my day at my internship.

The doubts, though, didn't leave me. They clung to me, a constant reminder of everything that was broken. The idea of breaking up with him lingered heavily in my mind, growing stronger with every moment that passed.

When we arrived at the brewery, the tension was palpable. Austin was unnervingly calm, far too relaxed for someone who was supposedly in a strained relationship. I could feel my anxiety building, and by the time I went to the bathroom, I was struggling to keep myself together. I stayed there for nearly twenty minutes, hoping to pull myself together.

But the tears wouldn't stop. Eventually, I forced myself to walk back out, expecting Austin to show at least a hint of concern.

Instead, he looked at me almost blankly, taking his time as he glanced around the gift shop, picking up a sweatshirt and examining it as if we had all the time in the world.

"I need to leave," I said, my voice wavering, barely able to hold back my frustration.

"Alright, just a sec," he replied, barely looking up as he continued browsing.

A new wave of anger surged through me. How could he be so indifferent? I was barely holding myself together, and he was acting as if nothing was wrong. "Austin, I'm serious," I snapped, feeling the tears starting to spill over again. "Can we go? Please?"

"Yeah, yeah, just let me pay for this real quick," he muttered, shrugging as if I was overreacting.

I watched in disbelief as he paid for his sweatshirt, then strolled back to the table and casually finished his beer. My chest felt tight, my hands shaking as I fought to keep myself from breaking down in front of everyone. But the weight of everything was too much.

Unable to hold back any longer, I grabbed his keys from the table and stormed out to the truck, leaving him to catch up. When he finally got to the truck, he looked at me, his expression exasperated.

"Lily, you need to calm down," he said, his voice laced with irritation. He turned the truck on, and we started driving back to his house.

For a few minutes, we bickered back and forth, our voices rising and falling in the confined space of the truck. Then, out of nowhere, he asked, "Do you want to break up again?"

I stared out the window, my chest tightening. "I don't know how to feel right now," I admitted, my voice trembling. "I'm not happy anymore, Austin. I'm not comfortable in this relationship. I can't sleep, I can't be out in public without crying about the thoughts of you hurting me again and everything you did to me."

He was silent for a moment, gripping the steering wheel tightly. Finally, he said, "If you can't move past what I did, then there's no point in being together."

All I wanted in that moment was for him to show that he cared—for him to fight for me, for us. I wanted him to tell me he'd do whatever it took to fix things, to make me feel safe again. But instead, it felt like the opposite. His words felt like a slap in the face, another reminder of how little he was willing to fight for me.

A few minutes later, the truck slowed as we hit a traffic jam caused by an accident ahead. We were stuck sitting there, at a standstill, for what felt like hours. My quiet sobs filled the silence.

"So this is it?" he finally said, breaking the silence. "We're done?"

I turned to look at him, tears streaming down my face. He didn't look at me; his gaze was fixed on the windshield. "I can't believe we're actually done," he muttered, almost to himself.

I sobbed quietly, unable to speak. He continued, his voice growing more desperate. "What about everything we talked about? All the dreams we had? The house, the trips, the life we planned together, the life we've been building. Are you really just going to throw all of that away?"

I couldn't answer him. The words caught in my throat as I tried to process the whirlwind of emotions crashing over me. His questions and all the things he said about our future made my mind flip. Once traffic started moving, it felt like my mind was racing at a million miles a minute. I kept asking myself: *Could I really break up with him? I still love him. Can I live without him?*

The confusion was overwhelming. My thoughts collided, spinning out of control. My chest felt tight, my vision blurring. "Pull over," I managed to say, clutching my head. "I… I can't breathe."

He glanced at me, annoyed. He pulled over to the side of the road as I swung the door open.

"This is ridiculous, Lily. Just get back in the truck."

My head spun as I grabbed onto the guardrail, trying to catch my breath. After a couple minutes, I managed to get back in the truck.

Once we finally reached his house, I couldn't hold it in any longer. As soon as we were parked, I turned to him, my voice breaking.

"What do you want from me, Austin? I can't keep doing this. I can't keep pretending everything's fine when it's not."

He looked back at me, his face unreadable. "What do you want to do, Lily?" he asked, his voice flat, almost indifferent. "Do you want to break up? Is that what this is?"

I felt a surge of frustration and sorrow rise up in me. "I don't want to lose you," I whispered, the words slipping out before I could stop them. "But I don't know how to keep going when everyday feels like another reminder of everything you've done to hurt me."

"You can't live without me; you're my person." He said, almost with a sad puppy dog look on his face.

At that moment, I thought, "I *can* live without you, I *want* a life with you, just a better version of you."

We sat in silence, the weight of my words filling the truck. And for a moment, I thought maybe he'd finally understand, perhaps he'd finally realize what I needed from him. But instead, he shrugged, his voice calm. "I don't know what you want me to do, Lil."

I let out a bitter laugh, the sound hollow even to my own ears. "I want you to care, Austin. I want you to care enough to stop hurting me, to actually try for once."

He turned to me, his face softening as he reached for my hand. "Lily, I do care. You know I care. I'm just not good at showing it, okay? I know I've messed up, but that doesn't mean I don't love you."

"Love isn't supposed to feel like this," I shot back, tears streaming down my face. "It's not supposed to hurt this much."

"I know," he said quietly, squeezing my hand. "And I hate that I've made you feel like this. I hate seeing you cry because of me. I just... I don't know how to fix it, but I want to. I want to try, for you, for us."

I looked away, my heart aching at the sound of his words. "You've said that before, Austin. You've said you'd try, but nothing ever changes."

He leaned closer, his voice pleading. "This time will be different. I promise. I'll be better. I'll prove it to you. Just give me one more chance, Lily. Please."

The desperation in his voice pulled at me, wrapping around my resolve like a vice. I wanted so badly to believe him, to believe that this time he meant it. That this time, things would really change.

"And what if it's not different?" I whispered, barely able to meet his eyes. "What if I give you another chance, and you just hurt me again?"

He shook his head, his voice firm. "I won't. I swear I won't. I can't lose you, Lily. You're my everything. You're the only good thing I have."

His words lingered in the air between us, filling the silence with their weight. And just like so many times before, he found a way to pull me back into the tangled web of his hold, leaving me caught between love and pain once again.

We left his house on Friday, spending the weekend at mine, trying to pretend everything was fine and hold onto whatever was left. The rest of the weekend, Austin was kinder, more loving, and unusually attentive. He was softer in his words, quick to laugh at my jokes, and more present with my family. He sat at the table during meals instead of retreating to his phone on the couch. He even complimented my mom's cooking and listened when my dad and brother talked about their latest car projects. For a fleeting moment, it felt like he was the version of Austin I had fallen in love with.

But deep down, I knew better. I could feel the unspoken tension hanging in the air. He wasn't being this way because he suddenly understood what I needed from him. He was performing, making sure my family saw the "right" version of him—the one he knew they needed to see, especially after everything they knew about us. It felt like a game, his way of trying to hold it all together before the cracks became too visible.

And as much as I wanted to believe it was real, I couldn't shake the feeling that it wasn't. His effort felt temporary, fragile, like it could crumble at any moment. And the weight of that realization sat heavy in my chest, reminding me that this version of him would never last.

# *Chapter*

# 18

# I Surrender

The screen flickered with his face, familiar but somehow distant. I could see the look of pain in his eyes. The exhaustion from the last three weeks of us going back and forth on what we should do about us. His eyes searched for mine, leaning forward slightly, as if looking closer might help him understand.

"You haven't been texting me much at all today." He paused. "Are we okay?" he asked, his voice carrying a mix of frustration, confusion, and something else—something closer to desperation. It was a tone I knew well, one he used when he didn't want to know the answer.

I took a deep breath, feeling the weight of words I'd held back for weeks. My heart raced, my hands trembling as I held the phone.

"I just… I feel like it's too late," I said, each word feeling like a step toward the edge of a cliff. His face fell, his expression shifting from anger to something softer, something vulnerable, as if he could sense the finality in my words.

"What do you mean it's too late? I thought we were trying to fix this. I thought you were going to give me a chance to prove to you that I wanted this. Now it's just… over?" he said, so fast and desperate, almost as if it was a reflex for him to speak. Like he was clinging to the only thing he knew how to do– keep talking, keep reaching, as if he could pull me back with his voice.

I hadn't planned for it to happen like this over the phone. I'd told myself that it needed to be in person, that I owed him that much. And I'd tried – twice. Each time, I'd find myself falling apart, crying in his arms, desperately trying to hold on even as I knew it was killing me. In those moments, walking away had felt impossible, like leaving would mean giving up on all the love and promises we'd built together. I hadn't been able to say goodbye then; each time, the idea of ending it in person had broken me, leaving me clinging to him even harder.

But tonight, as he pushed me for answers, something in me cracked open. Maybe I needed the distance from the screen, a barrier to shield me from the pull he'd always had on me. I took a deep breath,

"We've tried so many times," I continued, barely able to steady my voice. "I convince myself that you'll change, that things will be different. But every time we try, you just do the same things to hurt me, over and over again." I pause, "I'm exhausted Austin." I could see him processing, searching for a way to argue, to bring me back. But he couldn't, not this time.

"So that's it?" he asked, softer this time, his voice shaking. "It's really over?"

I felt my heart aching, shattering by the second. In-person, this moment might have broken me, or it might have pulled me back. But here, over the phone, I could finally see the truth laid bare: that I couldn't keep sacrificing myself for the hope that he might change.

"I just can't do this anymore," I said, feeling both the weight and the relief of those words.

"Everytime I stay, I lose a little more of myself trying to believe in something that keeps breaking. But I can't keep losing myself just to hold on to you. I'm tired of fighting, I'm tired of waiting around for the day you finally change."

He looked at me, tears rolled down his face. "Is there really nothing I can say?" he finally whispered, his voice barely audible. "Nothing I can do to make you stay?"

The truth is, I wished there was. Every time he had hurt me over the past three years, there was always a reason for me to stay. Three weeks ago, the reasons started to vanish. And at this point, I couldn't think of anything tying me to him anymore. Love just wasn't enough.

We'd been here before, in this same place, over and over, and each time, I was left with the pieces to put back together, as if I was the one who did the hurting.

"I'm sorry," I replied, my voice barely above a whisper. "But I can't keep doing this to myself. I have to let go."

There was nothing left to say. Slowly, he nodded, staring off into the distance of his room. I stared at his face, waiting for a reply.

"Well, I guess that's it then... I'm gonna go," he says sharply. "Goodbye, Lily."

"Bye Austin," I said, my voice steady as I forced the words out. The screen went black. I glanced at the clock–11:05 PM. The room fell silent, like a ringing in my ears, the kind of silence that comes when something you thought would never end is finally over.

I thought I'd feel relief, maybe even some sense of closure. Instead, the quiet felt heavier than I'd expected, an emptiness that lingered, like I'd left a part of myself in the space between us.

The room was still, almost suffocating, and all I could do was sit there, letting the finality of it sink in. It was over, really over, and there was nothing left to say, nothing more to hold onto.

The next morning, my phone was filled with messages from Austin; he told me he'd stayed home from work and couldn't pull himself together enough to go. And for a moment, I almost felt guilty. Almost. I could picture him there, lying in his bed, texting me with that same look he had last night on FaceTime—the look that wavered between anger and sadness, the same one that had kept me hanging on all those times before.

He kept asking why, over and over as if the reasons hadn't been spelled out a hundred times before. "Why can't we try again?" he asked, the words pleading and pushing, almost like he was searching for a loophole in the finality of it all.

I tried to answer, tried to explain yet again, but the words felt hollow. Nothing I said felt like enough for him to understand, to make him let go. And maybe that's the hardest part—knowing I can't make him see the truth, that I can't convince him to stop pushing, stop hoping that I'll give in again. I could feel him grasping at the pieces of me I'd left behind, trying to piece us back together, but I just... I can't.

I still wanted to keep texting him. Isn't that twisted? After all of this, there's a part of me that still craves that connection, even if it's tainted by all the hurt. Maybe it's a habit, or maybe it's just the loneliness kicking in faster than I'd prepared for. It's hard to turn off something that's been there for three years, especially when he's right there, just a message away, asking me to come back, making promises he can't keep.

But deep down, I know it's too late. Going back means erasing everything I've come to understand about myself, about him, about us. And yet, that doesn't make the silence any easier to bear. It feels like a hole I can't fill, no matter how many times I remind myself of why I left. I'm left here with an almost deafening quiet, wondering if he feels it too—or if he's already searching for someone else to fill the void I left behind.

# 19

# **Burning House**

Everyone talks about grief like it's a linear process, like you can check off the stages one by one—denial, anger, bargaining, depression, acceptance—and then, magically, you're healed. They make it sound like you'll feel a little less broken with each passing stage, like the pain will neatly dissolve as you progress toward the finish line of "moving on." But grief doesn't work like that. At least, it didn't for me.

For me, grief started with anger. Not sadness or disbelief, but pure, burning anger. I was angry at him for the lies, the broken promises, the ways he made me feel small. But more than that, I was angry at myself. Angry for staying as long as I did, for letting him fool me over and over again.

*How could I have been so stupid?* I thought, replaying every red flag I'd ignored, every time I forgave him when I shouldn't have. *How could I have let him treat me like that and convince myself it was love?*

During those days of processing everything, my mind kept circling back to little moments, things I had brushed off at the time but now seemed glaringly obvious. One memory in particular stood out. I had been working on a family tree project for class, tracing my own family's history, when Austin's family came up in conversation. His mom, Pam, had been keeping me company while Austin was at work. She started listing who had cheated in the family, rattling off names like it was a simple part of their history.

She talked about Austin's dad's side of the family—how they were close-knit in some ways, but not without their flaws.

"My dad cheated on my mom when I was growing up," she said matter-of-factly, her voice steady. "It was hard, but they stayed together."

I looked at her, unsure of what to say, and nodded as she continued. "And Austin's dad's father... he cheated too. And his grandfather before him. It's just... something that happened back then, I guess. The wives always stayed, though. That's how it was. Except for me," she added with a small, tight smile. "I couldn't do it. When Austin's dad cheated, I left. I wasn't going to let him treat me like that."

I hadn't thought much of it at the time—just another odd quirk of his family that didn't feel relevant to us. But now, as I sat there stewing in my anger, that conversation hit me like a slap in the face. *It was bound to happen*, I realized. *It's in his DNA.*

It wasn't just something Austin did. It was part of a pattern, a cycle that seemed to run through his family like an unspoken rule. And the more I thought about it, the more it infuriated me. *How could I have ever believed he'd be different?* I asked myself. *How could I have convinced myself that I'd be the exception?*

The anger consumed me in those early days, running through my mind on a constant loop. I was furious that I'd let myself believe in him, furious that I'd let him waste years of my life. Every time I thought about the lies he told or the way he dismissed my feelings, it felt like the fire inside me grew hotter.

It was during this time that the song *Burning House* by Cam became the soundtrack to my grief. The lyrics resonated so deeply, it felt as though they were written for me. *"I had a dream about a burning house, you were stuck inside, I couldn't get you out."* Those words echoed in my mind constantly, capturing the way Austin consumed my thoughts even when I tried to move forward.

He was everywhere—in my dreams, in the quiet moments of my day, in the memories that refused to fade. When I was sad, it wasn't just about losing my boyfriend; it was about losing my best friend, the person I had once turned to for everything. But I wasn't seeing him as he truly was. In my mind, he was still the version I wanted him to be, the one I had built up in my dreams.

The line, *"Love isn't all that it seems I did you wrong,"* hit me like a knife every time I heard it. Part of me felt like I had failed too—failed to fix us, failed to see the truth earlier, failed to be enough to make him change. But the hardest line to hear was *"I stay here with you."* Because that was exactly what I was doing—staying in the wreckage of our relationship, holding onto the pain as if it were the only way to hold onto him.

The song wasn't just about loss; it was about the way grief traps you in a place where moving forward feels impossible. It mirrored the push and pull of my emotions—the longing to escape the fire, but also the fear of what life would look like without it.

But anger isn't sustainable. It burns brightly for a while, but eventually, it gives way to something else. For me, that something else was sadness. The kind of sadness that sits heavy on your chest, making it hard to breathe. The kind that catches you off guard in the middle of the day, leaving you in tears without warning. It was the sadness of realizing that the future I had imagined with him—the future I had built my life around—was gone.

Even then, the grief didn't follow any neat, predictable pattern. One day, I'd feel strong, like I was finally ready to move on, to start fresh and leave him behind. The next day, I'd feel the disbelief creeping in, whispering, *Did we really break up? Is it really over?*

Grief wasn't just about losing him. It was about losing the version of myself I thought I was in our relationship. I had convinced myself that I was strong, that I was resilient, that I could handle anything. But the truth was, I had been breaking piece by piece, sacrificing parts of myself to keep us together. And now that it was over, I was left to pick up the pieces and figure out who I was without him.

There were moments of hope, too—glimpses of what life could be like without the weight of our relationship holding me down. I'd catch myself smiling at the thought of starting over, of creating a life that was truly mine. But those moments were fleeting, often overshadowed by the memories of him and the life we had planned together.

What no one tells you about grief is that it doesn't end. It shifts, it changes, but it never fully disappears. It becomes a part of you, a scar that fades with time but never truly goes away. For me, grief was a reminder of how deeply I had loved, how much I had given, and how much I had grown. And while it was painful, it was also proof that I had survived.

### Thursday, April 18, 2024

*Well, It's been almost four months since my last journal entry. We broke up. To be more specific, I broke up with Austin for the last time on Tuesday, April 16. We broke up twice before this, a week or two before I officially broke up with him. Honestly, I'm surprised it wasn't more than that in the three years we've been together.*

*I miss him, but I know I only miss the part of him that I created in my head. The person I knew he could be but never put the time in to change. I know that I can't change someone, and I have spent so long waiting around for him to want to change for me. I don't regret dating him because it taught me a lot about what I need in a relationship and what I deserve.*

*I regret spending as much time as I did in this relationship; how much time I spent neglecting myself. I wish I had the courage to do it earlier. You know what they say, everything happens for a reason. He meant everything to me, and I put him first in every scenario of my life. It's hard letting that go. All the plans we made, dreams we shared. But it's kind of exciting getting to plan my future for me.*

*It's also terrifying. I'm scared I won't find someone who meets my needs. I know no one is perfect, but I want someone who makes me happier than I've ever been, someone who will make me a priority, who's loyal, and who would never hurt me.*

*I pray I heal from the hurt he caused me. Looking back, I knew I'd never be able to forgive him and forget about the things he did to me or said about me behind my back. I was holding on to something that was never meant for me.*

*I hate how I feel about him now. He was never someone I'd thought I'd ever hate. But I do, I really do hate him. I hate him for lying to me, hurting me, breaking my heart, breaking promises, and breaking me. Yes, I was the one who broke up with him, but he hurt me first.*

*I hope I'll be able to love again to my fullest potential. I hope it doesn't shatter me when he starts dating someone else. I hope I can be happy and find a purpose for myself. I still think about him constantly, but the stress and anxiety are gone because I'm no longer worried about what he's doing behind my back or that he'll hurt me again. I just hope that I can move on from this; it gets better every day.*

*I wish it was meant to be him, just a better version of him.*

~ ~ ~

Grieving Austin wasn't just about letting go of him. It was about letting go of the dreams we had shared, the life I thought we would build, and the version of love I had clung to for so long. It was about learning to forgive myself for staying as long as I did and for loving someone who couldn't love me the way I deserved. And, most importantly, it was about learning to love myself again—to believe that I am worthy of the kind of love I spent so long hoping he would give me.

Grief isn't one-size-fits-all. It's messy, unpredictable, and deeply personal. And for me, it was a reminder that healing isn't about erasing the pain—it's about learning to carry it with you, one day at a time.

*Chapter*

# 20

# Breaking More Hearts Than Mine

The drive to my internship felt longer than usual, the hour stretching out as I thought about everything that happened. I've been doing an internship with social workers at Austin's mom's work. I just have three weeks left. I'd been okay for the most part–maybe even a little relieved. But all I could think about was seeing his mom, Pam. She'd been off from work on Thursday, and I knew facing her would make everything feel more real.

When I walked into the office, she was already crying. I dropped my bag as soon as I saw her, and before I could say anything, we were hugging. I could feel her shoulders shaking, her own sadness blending with mine, and suddenly, I was crying, too. The calm I'd felt about the breakup was gone, replaced by an ache I hadn't expected.

"I'm so sorry," she whispered, pulling back to look at me. "Are you... are you okay?"

I nodded, trying to find the words. "I'll be okay."

Throughout the day, I found myself back in the office, each visit a reminder of what I'd lost–not just Austin, but my relationship with Pam. She handed me a small gift in the morning, a birthday present she'd planned before any of this happened. We sat together at lunch, talking quietly, and she finally asked, "Is it really over?"

I hesitated, not wanting to hurt her any more than I already had. "Yes… for now," I replied, the words hanging in the air between us. Part of me didn't want to admit that it was over for good, even though I knew it was. I couldn't bring myself to say that out loud–not to her, and not to myself. So I left the door open, even though, deep down, I knew I'd already closed it.

She looked at me with a mixture of sadness and hope. "He asked if I'd seen you," she said, her voice soft. "He wanted to know if you looked happy."

I forced a small smile, knowing she'd told him I didn't look happy. It was easier for him to think that, easier for us to pretend that the hurt was mutual. But the truth was, I was starting to feel lighter. It was just hard to let her see that.

I opened her gift to find a pair of gold butterfly earrings. Pam knew well about my love for butterflies, but these carried a meaning she may not have fully realized. In 2021, six months after Austin and I started dating, I lost my grandmother, my Nonnie. That year was a whirlwind–falling in love while grieving one of the hardest losses of my life.

The day before she passed, I was at Austin's house, sitting with him outside. Out of nowhere, a blue and black butterfly floated toward me. It allowed me to pick it up and wouldn't fly away until I placed it back down. Since that moment, butterflies have always reminded me of her, a quiet sign that she's still with me, watching over me. And now, here they were again, a parting gift from Pam. Somehow, it felt like one last reminder of everything I was now letting go.

I closed the box gently, offering Pam a smile and a hug, though a familiar heaviness lingered. As I went back and forth to the office all day, it felt like I was watching my relationship with her crumble. I realized that, in a way, I was saying goodbye to the life I'd imagined, a future that had once felt so full of promise.

As my birthday approached, I found myself letting go of that vision, too. It was a day I'd once planned to spend by his side, a day I'd hoped he'd make special until I understood how often I'd been holding onto hopes he never quite fulfilled.

*Friday, April 19, 2024*

*Today was a day filled with so much emotion. It's only been a few days since I ended things with Austin, and I'm already feeling the weight of everything, but today was especially heavy. It's the anniversary of my PopPop's death, and somehow, in the midst of all this hurt, I felt him and Nonnie with me. Their presence felt strong, almost like they were wrapping me up, reminding me that I'm not alone.*

*When I opened the box with the butterfly earrings from Pam this morning, it was like a sign—a reminder from Nonnie that she's still here, still watching over me. Butterflies have always made me feel close to her, especially since the day I lost her. But today, I felt Pop, too, like they were both with me, guiding me through all this pain. It gave me a strange comfort, like they're telling me it's okay to let go, that they'll be there to hold me up.*

*It's hard to accept that I'm really walking away from the future I'd dreamed up with Austin, but feeling them with me today somehow made it easier to believe in a different path, one that's still full of love and strength. I miss them so much, but knowing they're here, reminding me of what I deserve, makes me feel just a little less alone.*

*Chapter*

# 21

# The Cherry on Top

As my birthday approached, I tried not to think about the plans Austin and I had discussed. It was supposed to be my first birthday away from my family, a night I'd planned to spend with him. We had talked about making it special–a small celebration, nothing extravagant, just the two of us. I'd told him what mattered to me, hoping he'd understand. A cake, maybe a dinner somewhere nice. Simple things, but meaningful.

But every time I asked if he'd called to order the cake or make a reservation, he brushed me off. "Stop nagging, I'll get to it," he'd say with a hint of impatience, as if my birthday was just another item on his to-do list. I reminded myself not to take it personally, yet deep down, I knew how often I'd been disappointed. For his birthdays, I'd gone out of my way, planning dinners and making pies and ice cream cakes over the years since he didn't like cake. Organizing a surprise party with his friends and family. Each year, I made sure he felt celebrated. I wanted him to know he was special to me.

With him, though, it always felt like I was asking for too much. I'd given him step-by-step instructions for ordering the cake, three options of what he could get and where to get it from, and all he'd have to do was pick one. Still, as the date got closer, he hadn't made a single call.

I stopped asking eventually, feeling a strange calm settle in. By then, it was too late for a cake to change anything. My birthday was the last thing on my mind.

The morning of my birthday came, and I was home with my family. It was comforting, the familiar warmth of waking up in my own house, the smell of my dad's espresso drifting up the stairs from the kitchen, and my parents' voices filling the spaces where his absence felt sharpest.

I reached over and grabbed my phone, noticing a message from after midnight, "I know I'm probably the last person you want to hear from, but I just wanted to wish you a happy birthday." He'd written. "I got you a cake. I can give it to you tomorrow when you come get your stuff. Though, I wish we could enjoy it together."

I stared at the message, frustration bubbling up inside me. I could imagine him expecting me to be grateful for this last-minute gesture as if it could somehow erase all the ways he'd let me down. It was the cherry on top, the final reminder of just how tired I was of chasing after his half-efforts, his empty promises. Here he was, offering the cake as if it was a peace offering, yet it felt hollow—more for his benefit than mine.

I replied that I didn't need it. I already had a cake, and I was spending the day with people who didn't need reminders or step-by-step guides to make me feel valued. The birthday passed quietly, filled with love and support from the ones who mattered. With each hour that went by, I felt a bit of the weight lift, realizing that the only expectations I needed to fulfill were my own.

That night, after brushing off Austin's message, my phone buzzed again. This time, it was from his older friend, Blake, reaching out on Snapchat to wish me a happy birthday. I hesitated before opening it, not really in the mood for another conversation that reminded me of him. But I figured I'd be polite, so I replied with a quick thank you, hoping that would be the end of it.

Instead, he kept messaging me, casually mentioning that he'd heard from Austin. "He told me you guys were going through a rough patch," Blake said, describing it as if it was some minor setback. A small wave of irritation flared up in me.

Rough patch? I thought. I'd broken up with him. I wasn't about to let anyone downplay what I'd been through, so I replied, "Actually, I broke up with him."

There was a pause, and I thought that might finally end the conversation. Blake asked, "What happened?" Without giving him too much information—frankly, it's none of his business—I gave him a few reasons. Blake's tone shifted. He called me beautiful, mentioning how if I were his, he'd never treat me this way. I was taken aback, unsure how to respond. Part of me wanted to roll my eyes at the sudden flattery, and part of me felt the weight of irony–one of Austin's friends hitting on me just days after I'd cut things off.

I brushed off his comments, making a quick excuse to end the chat. It was just another reminder that I'd made the right decision. Austin hadn't even been honest with his friends about the breakup, and here was one of them trying to swoop in, as if I hadn't just been through three years of trying to make things work with someone who couldn't see my worth.

*Chapter*

# 22

# Closing the Distance

The following Thursday, after working at my internship for the day, I drove to his house to pick up my things. As I pulled up, I noticed something strange—he'd shaved his beard, mustache, everything. He hadn't been clean-shaven in two years, and now, suddenly, he was. It felt like some kind of display, as if he thought it might change my mind.

He stood there waiting, his eyes sad and searching, as I stepped out of the car with a quick "Hey." I went straight to the trunk to grab his things, hoping to make this quick, but before I could say anything, he asked, "Is this really what you want?"

I took a deep breath, bracing myself. "Can we just exchange our stuff first? Then we can talk."

He nodded, but even once we were inside, he didn't stop. He kept asking questions, as if repeating them would somehow change my answer. I felt the weight of his gaze on me as I moved throughout his room, gathering up my things and stuffing them into a bag. Every item I picked up seemed to bring back a memory—things that had once felt like pieces of a life we were building together were now just reminders of how much I needed to leave.

He followed me to each corner of the room, hovering close like he was afraid that if he didn't stay near, I'd disappear. His presence was constant, his questions bleeding together into a murmur of desperation that I tried to ignore. I kept telling myself, "Stay strong. Don't let him get in your head." But with every look, every pleading question, it was like he was reaching for pieces of me I'd already let go of.

As I stuffed the last of my things into the bag, I felt the tension building inside me. I just wanted this to end. I made my way to the door, but he stepped in front of me, his face full of that same unrelenting question.

"You haven't answered me," he said quietly, like it was the last thing keeping us together. "Is this really what you want?"

I forced myself to meet his gaze. "I'm tired of not being a priority in your life," I replied, my voice steady but firm. "All I've ever done is make you number one in mine, and I can't keep doing that."

We went back and forth, his words blending into a blur as he tried again and again to pull me back. I kept my focus, repeating to myself that I was done and couldn't keep losing myself to someone who never saw my worth.

I finally gathered my bag and headed outside, hoping for a quick exit. But he followed me, trailing behind like a shadow. As I loaded my things into the car, he walked around to the other side, blocking my way. "I guess this is it," he said, his voice barely more than a whisper.

"Yeah... unfortunately it is," I replied, the words sinking in, creating a silence that felt like the last page of a story neither of us wanted to keep reading.

"It doesn't have to be this way," he murmured, his tone almost pleading.

"Yes it does Austin," I replied, meeting his gaze one last time. "I can't do this anymore. It's over."

He asked for a hug, and I obliged, feeling him hold on a little too long, as if he were trying to make this last moment count. When I pulled back, he looked at me with a glimmer of hope, as if he could still convince me. But I took a step back, got into my car, and closed the door.

He stood leaning against his truck directly in front of me, watching as I started the engine. I took a deep breath, glanced at him one last time, and shifted into reverse, backing down the driveway. He raised a hand in a small wave, his eyes glassy with unshed tears. I didn't wave back. Instead, I put the car in drive and pulled away, watching him grow smaller in the rearview mirror until he disappeared from sight.

## Thursday, April 25, 2024

*Driving away felt surreal, like I was leaving a piece of myself behind in his driveway. I kept my eyes forward, even though every instinct screamed to look back. This quiet, heavy ache settled in, and yet, beneath it, there was relief—a small, fragile sense of freedom I hadn't felt in so long.*

*Seeing him like that—clean-shaven, watching me with that look—was harder than I expected. I don't know if he really thought shaving his face or saying all the right things could somehow rewind time, erase the hurt, or make me forget the pain. But I knew better. I'd held onto hope for too long, hoping each time he would change.*

*He kept asking me, over and over, "Is this really what you want?" It was like he couldn't believe I'd actually reached this point. But each question only made me hold tighter to my decision, reminding me why I had to choose myself this time. I had to remind myself that his words and promises had only ever been temporary band-aids on wounds that were never going to heal. No matter how much his sadness mirrored my own, I couldn't let myself be pulled back.*

*The way he looked at me, the way he reached for one last hug, it tore at me. Part of me wanted to believe that maybe, this time, he was serious. That maybe, if I gave him one last chance, things would be different. But I knew that was just the part of me that didn't want to let go, the part that remembered our good moments, the times he did make me feel special. Those moments, though, were never enough to outweigh the pain.*

*I can feel the emptiness he's left behind. It's strange how a person can take up so much space in your life, and then suddenly, they're gone, and you're left with this quiet, aching void. But I also feel something else—a sense of peace, however faint. I know this is going to be hard, that loneliness will hit like waves, but I have to believe I'll come out stronger.*

*It hurts, but I know this was right.*

*Chapter*

# 23

# Learning to Be Alone

The second weekend without him hit harder. The previous weekend, I had buried myself in the comfort of my family. My mom and I took a trip to Annapolis, Maryland, with my cousins and aunts to celebrate our moms' 60th birthdays. It was exactly what I'd needed, filled with laughter, celebration, and those rare moments where everything felt normal, almost like a reset button. My family's warmth and support helped me talk through things and reminded me I wasn't as alone as I felt. I was up and down all weekend, the joy often tinged with this unsettling nausea every time I remembered he wasn't there, that I'd chosen to finally let him go.

But now, back in my own routine, the reality of being without him fully settled in. Weekends were starting to feel hollow, like a constant, silent ache was sitting just beneath the surface. There was an empty space where he used to be, and no matter how I tried to fill it—with friends, errands, projects, anything to distract myself—his absence was there, lingering, woven into everything around me. It was strange; I'd been the one to end things, but the ache still surfaced. It was as if, even though I'd let him go, I couldn't entirely escape his hold.

Part of me tried to take control, to draw my own boundaries. Blocking him on TikTok was my attempt to reclaim a sense of distance, a small but necessary step after he'd already blocked me everywhere else. I thought that by cutting him off completely, I could start to feel more in control of the situation, like it would finally give me the space I needed to heal. But it only made things feel messier. Pam, his mom, kept viewing my profile, popping up on my notifications. I couldn't make sense of it—was she looking for something, trying to keep tabs on me, or just as unable to let go as I was?

At my internship, she'd been distant, too, her warmth replaced by a quiet coldness I couldn't ignore. I tried to push it aside, to tell myself it was bound to happen, but it stung to see the shift. She was a constant reminder of him, of the life we'd built around each other, and now even that had turned into something foreign and painful. Where her presence had once been a source of comfort, now it reminded me of how much everything had changed.

Sometimes, I wished I'd been the one to block him first, that I'd had the strength to sever those ties before he had. It was a small thing, really, but it felt like a reflection of just how easily he'd let go of us. But it was so difficult for him to block the many other girls he talked to throughout our relationship—girls he'd promised me he'd cut off but never did. For years, I was the one holding us together, ensuring we didn't fall apart, even when he didn't seem willing to do the same. And now that it was over, I was left with questions that felt impossible to answer. Why did he hurt me? Why did this have to be another painful lesson, just another chapter of betrayal and heartbreak?

Despite knowing I was better off, the ache lingered, and so did the fear—that quiet, creeping fear that maybe I'd never find someone who sees my worth, who values me for who I truly am. The world felt empty in those moments, my thoughts circling around the same questions, the same doubt. I knew it was irrational, that there were people out there who would love me differently, but it didn't stop the fear from sinking in, from making itself at home in my mind.

It was time for a change. I had to believe that healing was possible, that the future held something better than what I'd lost. But right now, that belief was thin, wavering under the weight of everything I was feeling. I was lost, but I was also hopeful, clinging to the tiny bit of faith

I had left, praying that this emptiness would pass. Maybe, in time, I'd be strong enough to fill that space with something real, something that was finally mine.

### Sunday, April 28, 2024

*Weekends feel hollow now. There's this empty space where he used to be, and no matter how I try to fill it—with people, plans, distractions—it's like a part of him lingers. Even though I chose to end things, the ache still surfaces, and I keep catching myself looking for traces of him in the life I'm piecing back together.*

*Blocking him on TikTok should have felt like taking control. After he'd blocked me everywhere else, I thought it would help create some distance. I even blocked his parents, hoping it would stop the constant reminders. But somehow, it only made things messier. Pam keeps checking my profile, as if she's looking for something. At my internship, she's been distant, and it's hard not to feel that loss, too. What was once a comfortable part of my life has turned into a reminder of all that's changed.*

*Sometimes, I wish I'd been the one to block him first. It's a small thing, but it's hard not to see it as a reflection of how easily he let go of us. But it was so difficult for him to block the many other girls he talked to throughout our relationship—girls he promised me he'd cut off but never did. For years, I was the one making us work, holding us together even when he couldn't. And now that it's over, I can't help but wonder why it had to end this way—why it hurts so deeply to walk away from someone who couldn't hold on to me.*

*I keep asking myself why it still stings. I know, logically, that I'm better off, but it doesn't change the questions that keep coming back. Why did he hurt me? Why did this have to be yet another lesson? And there's this quiet fear in me, too, that maybe I'll never find someone who values me for who I am. It's a fear I can't shake, even though I know it's irrational.*

*It's time for a change. I'm putting my faith in the belief that I'll heal, that better things are waiting. Right now, though, I just feel lost. I'm scared but hopeful, too, praying that this emptiness won't last forever and that, in time, I'll be strong enough to fill it with something better.*

*Chapter*

## 24

# Social Isolation

After breaking things off with Austin, I thought life would start to feel different right away, like a new door opening to something better. For a while, it did. I felt a sense of relief like a weight had finally been lifted, and I could breathe on my own again. But once the initial rush of freedom faded, there was this other feeling that started creeping in—one I couldn't ignore. Isolation. As much as I was moving forward, it felt like I was walking through life on autopilot, doing the same thing day in and day out, and everything around me seemed to lose its color.

I started a new job, which kept me busy during the day. It was something I looked forward to—a change, a new chapter to focus on. The routine gave me a sense of purpose and each morning, I'd convince myself that this was exactly what I needed to keep moving forward. But as soon as I clocked out and drove home, the silence was there waiting, filling every corner of my life that used to be filled with plans, calls, and texts from Austin.

My friends, as supportive as they were, had their own lives. They had their own relationships, jobs, and responsibilities, and I didn't want to intrude or be the one who constantly needed them. I tried to keep myself occupied with work and hobbies, but everything felt repetitive like I was just going through the motions. Even though I didn't miss

Austin himself, there was this undeniable void. I'd spent so long filling my days with him, with his friends, with their plans. Now, I was filling that space with endless days at work, nights on my own, and a growing sense of loneliness.

It didn't help that I still saw him, even if it was only in glimpses. Austin's friends were active on social media, always posting videos of their nights out. I'd scroll through, half-tempted to ignore it but unable to look away. I'd see clips of him out with the same group, laughing, drinking, surrounded by people who seemed to have all the time in the world. And there he'd be, drink in hand, looking like he was living his best life without a second thought about me. They'd post about their weekend plans, stories full of girls, late nights, and parties. It hurt, but at the same time, it didn't. I didn't want that lifestyle anymore. I didn't want to be a part of those empty nights, waiting for him to decide I was enough to come home to.

I found some peace in knowing that I wasn't there anymore, that I wasn't out getting drunk every night or waiting for someone else to define my happiness. But even with that sense of relief, I couldn't ignore the loneliness that seemed to settle deeper every time I saw those posts. I didn't miss the relationship with him, but I missed the company, the routine, the sense of belonging—even if it was something that was hurting me. I'd taken steps forward, but the emptiness was a quiet reminder of everything I'd lost, even if what I lost was a version of myself I was glad to leave behind.

Some nights, it felt like I was moving backward instead of forward. I knew I was better off, but being alone was harder than I'd expected. The loneliness wasn't about wanting him back; it was about learning to fill the silence he left. I kept telling myself that this was just a phase, that I'd adjust. But each time I sat alone in my room, I couldn't help but wonder if I'd ever truly feel whole on my own.

### Monday, May 13, 2024

*Some days are harder than others. I thought this was going to get easier. I thought I'd be able to shake the loneliness by now, but here I am, still staring at my ceiling some nights, wondering if this empty feeling will ever go away.*

*I know I don't want him back. It's not about that—I've come too far to want that. But the silence is louder than I ever thought it would be.*

*Starting this job was supposed to fill the void and give me something to keep me moving. And it has, for the most part. During the day, I feel almost like myself again. I'm busy, I have a purpose, a reason to get out of bed. But once I'm back home, it's like all of that just fades. I go through the same motions, day after day, trying to convince myself that this is what healing looks like.*

*I saw another video of Austin out with his friends tonight, surrounded by girls and drinks. He looks happy—at least, he looks like he thinks he's happy. It doesn't hurt like it used to; I don't miss that version of us. But it does remind me that he's not alone. He has people around him, even if they're not the kind of people I want in my life. And here I am, feeling like I'm fighting this battle on my own.*

*I want to be okay with being alone. I want to feel like I don't need anyone to fill the silence. I'm trying, but right now, it just feels like a long stretch of nights with no end in sight. Part of me hopes that this is just another step in the process, that one day, I'll look back on this and feel proud for making it through. Right now, though, it's just me and the emptiness, and I don't know which one of us is winning.*

*Chapter*

# 25

# The Swipe That Stung

In a moment of loneliness last night, I decided to dip my toes into an old world—dating apps. It wasn't about finding anyone serious or even looking for anything at all. After months of unraveling from Austin, I just wanted a reminder that there were people beyond him, that I wasn't stuck in this endless cycle of wondering if I'd made the right choice. Part of me hoped that seeing new faces and exchanging a few light messages would soften the ache I'd been carrying around and maybe reassure me that I could move on.

Setting up my Bumble profile felt strange but oddly empowering. I'd spent so much time feeling lost, wondering if I'd ever find someone again or if he had been the only person who would ever see me that way. Swiping through strangers' profiles felt like a small step forward, even if it was just for a moment. It was harmless, I told myself. A little reminder that my world wasn't confined to memories of him.

The next morning, I woke up feeling a little bolder, a little more ready to face the day. I opened the app, swiping casually, hoping for a simple distraction. And then, the notification popped up: someone had liked my profile. Curious, I clicked—and there he was.

Austin.

It was like a gut punch, seeing his face, his name. My ex, the one I was trying to move on from, was right there, showing up in the one space I'd tried to claim for myself. Before I could even process the hurt bubbling up, I took a screenshot, sent it to him, and, against every instinct, I added: "Wow, that was fast."

He didn't miss a beat. His reply was as sharp as mine: "Same for you."

Anger surged through me. I knew things were over between us—of course, I did. But a selfish part of me, the part still nursing old wounds, hoped he'd be in too much pain to move on, at least not this quickly. He was the one who hurt me, who broke my trust over and over again. Seeing him there, swiping casually like none of it mattered, felt like a slap in the face.

But then again, why was I surprised? He'd done this while we were dating, hadn't he? That night with Kayla lingered in my mind, the words she'd said to Morgan cutting deeper than any fight we'd had. She'd told Morgan he wasn't happy with me, that he'd been complaining. For weeks after that, I couldn't shake the suspicion, the nagging feeling that there was more he wasn't telling me. Not long after, I'd found the emails on his phone—emails showing he'd downloaded Tinder, Bumble, and even paid for OnlyFans, all around the time she'd made that comment.

I threw his own words back at him now, words he'd once used to justify his behavior: "I'm going to focus on myself." The same words he'd promised me after we broke up, claiming he'd "work on himself" and "be better." I'd clung to those empty words, holding them close like they were a lifeline, some hope that he was truly remorseful. But seeing him on Bumble felt like the final confirmation. Every promise he'd made, every apology—it was all hollow, just words he'd used to keep me from walking away sooner.

Our conversation quickly spiraled into a messy argument, texts flying back and forth, each one more cutting than the last. I told him everything I hadn't had the courage to say before—how betrayed I'd felt, how humiliating it had been to find out he'd turned to dating apps and OnlyFans, even while he was telling me he loved me. As I watched his responses, a painful realization settled in: I was letting him hurt me again. I'd put myself back in the line of fire, hoping, somehow, that he'd finally understand, that he'd finally admit to the pain he'd caused.

But why would he?

I blocked him on Bumble, deleted the app, and told myself I was done with this mess. He said he'd delete it too, but the words felt as hollow as all the others. I ended our conversation on slightly better terms, but I couldn't stop myself from asking one last thing, hoping he might finally say something real. "What if I wanted to try again and found out you were on a dating app?" I asked, my last attempt to get through to him.

His response was as casual as it was cutting: "Then I'd delete it." And that was it. It all clicked into place. The broken promises, the lies, the betrayals—they'd been staring me in the face all along. He wasn't someone I could trust, not with the little things, not with the big things. And maybe I wasn't perfect either; I'd downloaded the app, too. But I hadn't done it behind his back while we were together, and I hadn't made promises I didn't intend to keep.

As I sat there alone, I felt a strange mix of relief and hurt. I knew I shouldn't have texted him, that reaching out had only reopened wounds I was still healing from. But deep down, it felt good to say it all, to yell at him one last time, to remind myself why I'd walked away. Yet, a sharp fear lingered, one I couldn't shake: What if he wasn't the one, but no one else would be either?

### Wednesday, May 29, 2024

*It's strange how easily I slipped back into old habits, back into anger and hurt. I thought yelling at him would bring me closure, that seeing him on that app would finally feel like a clean break. But here I am, still feeling the same ache.*

*Maybe it's the fear that's getting to me, this nagging worry that I won't find someone else—that maybe he was my only shot, and that's why letting go is so hard. I tried to move on, to take that small step forward, but instead, I feel emptier than before. Seeing him on the app felt like a confirmation, like he was right there, moving on with his life, leaving me to pick up the pieces on my own.*

*Sometimes, I wonder if there's something wrong with me, something that keeps me stuck in this hollow feeling. It's not just about being single; it's about this sense of isolation, this feeling that I'm drifting further away from everyone around me. I know I shouldn't let it get to me.*

*I've made progress; I've learned to stand on my own. But tonight, all I can see is this endless loop of trying, failing, and healing, each time leaving me a little more worn, a little more doubtful.*

*I miss companionship, but the thought of opening up to someone new feels exhausting, like a risk I can't afford to take. And yet, I'm lonely. I tell myself I need this time to grow, to find out who I am without him. But right now, all I feel is lost, wondering if there's really anything out there worth the pain of finding it.*

# Dancing on My Own

The combined bachelor and bachelorette weekend for Nick and Sophie was something I had been looking forward to for weeks. Planning the theme, decorations, and details had been a labor of love, and I wanted everything to be perfect for them. It was a chance to celebrate my brother and his fiancée and, for me, to escape my everyday routine. After everything I'd been through, I needed this—a weekend of laughter, fun, and a little breathing room from my thoughts.

When we arrived at the rental house, the atmosphere was already buzzing. The decorations I'd spent hours preparing were exactly as I envisioned—festive and vibrant. Sophie hugged me tightly, her eyes lighting up as she looked around. "Lily, this is amazing! You outdid yourself."

"I wanted you and Nick to have the best time," I said, smiling. "You deserve it."

Nick walked in, shaking his head with a grin. "Lily, seriously, you crushed this. Thanks for making this weekend so special."

"Anything for you guys," I replied. It felt good to focus on them and their happiness. For the first time in a while, I felt like I was contributing to something joyful.

One night during the trip, we were all gathered around the fire pit when Mark, one of Nick's friends, turned to me. "Hey, Lily, I'm not sure if you still follow Austin, but... did you see his Instagram post?"

The mention of Austin's name felt like a slap in the face. "No," I said carefully. "I unfollowed him a while ago. Why?"

Mark hesitated, glancing at Nick before pulling out his phone. "He got into an accident. He posted about it earlier this week."

He handed me his phone, and there it was—Austin's post. The picture showed the damages from the accident. The caption was vague but mentioned how lucky he was that no one was hurt.

I handed the phone back, forcing a neutral expression. "That's... crazy," I said, my voice steadier than I felt. "I'm glad he's okay."

Mark looked at me curiously. "What happened between you two? You guys seemed solid."

Nick shot him a warning look, but I shook my head. "It's fine," I said. "He did some things to me... it just wasn't working anymore."

Another one of Nick's friends, Ryan, chimed in. "Wait, Austin? What happened?"

I gave them the spark notes version. "There was a lot of dishonesty," I said simply. "I gave him a lot of chances, and he broke my trust too many times. It was hard, but it was the right thing to do."

The group fell silent for a moment before Nick said, "Alright, let's not make this weekend about him." He gave me a small smile, and I nodded, grateful for the way he always had my back.

Later that night, we went out to a club, the music pumping and the energy electric. I was determined to have fun, to let loose for once. As I stood by the bar with Lina and Sophie, sipping a cocktail, I noticed a guy across the room looking at me. He was tall, with an easy smile and dark, tousled hair. When our eyes met, I quickly looked away, feeling a blush rise to my cheeks.

Sophie nudged me. "He's cute," she said with a grin. "And he's totally checking you out."

"Stop," I said, laughing nervously. "It's nothing."

"Nothing?" Lina teased. "Lily, he hasn't taken his eyes off you since we got here. Go talk to him!"

Before I could protest, the guy started walking toward me. My stomach fluttered with nerves I hadn't felt in a long time. When he reached us, he smiled, his voice warm and confident. "Hi," he said, his gaze locking on mine. "I'm Braden."

"Lily," I replied, trying not to blush again.

"You look like you're having a good time," he said, leaning in slightly to be heard over the music.

"I am," I said, smiling. "It's been a while since I've had a night like this."

We started talking, and the conversation flowed easily. He asked about the bridal party, and I told him about Nick and Sophie's upcoming wedding. "That's awesome," he said. "Sounds like you put a lot of effort into making this weekend special for them."

"I did," I admitted. "But it's worth it. They're my favorite couple."

"They're lucky to have you," he said, his smile genuine.

His friends eventually joined our group, and everyone started mingling. As the drinks flowed and the music played, Braden turned to me again. "Want to dance?"

I hesitated for a moment, but Sophie gave me a little nudge. "Go!" she whispered.

I nodded, letting him lead me to the dance floor. The bass thumped around us as we moved to the music, and for the first time in months, I felt carefree. Braden twirled me around, making me laugh, and when he leaned in to say something, I caught the faint scent of his cologne— clean and warm. "You're a good dancer," he said with a grin.

"You're not so bad yourself," I replied, feeling a bit more at ease.

As we danced, the space between us grew smaller, and I felt a flicker of something I hadn't felt in a long time. It was strange, being so close to someone who wasn't Austin, but it also felt... liberating.

Toward the end of the song, he leaned in, his face close to mine. "Can I kiss you?" he asked, his voice barely above the music.

I froze for a moment, caught off guard by the question, but then I nodded. "Yeah," I said softly.

The kiss was gentle and sweet, not rushed or overwhelming. It was simple—no grand fireworks, no overwhelming emotions—but in its simplicity, it felt safe. It was a reminder that there was still something out there for me, even if I wasn't ready for it yet.

When we pulled back, he smiled. "You're amazing, you know that?"

I laughed softly, feeling a warmth I hadn't felt in months.

"Thanks, Braden."

We danced a little longer before returning to our groups. Braden's friends were joking with Nick and the bridal party, and for the rest of the night, the energy stayed light and fun.

When I got back to the rental house later, I couldn't help but replay the moment in my mind. Kissing someone who wasn't Austin felt like stepping into a new world—strange, but freeing. It wasn't about Braden, really; it was about realizing that I could move forward, even if it was just for a moment. For the first time in months, I felt like maybe, just maybe, I was going to be okay.

*Chapter*

# 27

## Finding My Way Back

The summer months had been a quiet blur of change. Life feels different, but in a way that I can't fully put into words yet. Early August brought a chance to break away for a while—I went to Georgia for my brother's best friend's wedding. What started as a weekend celebration turned into a much-needed road trip with Alyssa and my family, winding our way through Chattanooga, Nashville, and Memphis. Alyssa was exactly who I needed by my side: someone who knows how to make me laugh, who brings out the side of me that I haven't seen in a while. It was a week of laughter, music, and moments of lightness that I'd been craving.

There were moments, though, when memories of Austin would slip into my mind—like little shadows reminding me of a time I thought he'd be there with me. But every time he crossed my mind, I found myself grounded by a new kind of clarity. I knew that if Austin had been there, the trip would have likely turned into something entirely different.

I'd have to be constantly looking out for him, waiting for the inevitable moments he'd be either drunk or hungover, nursing him back to life while missing out on the experience myself. Realizing this became an anchor, helping me stay in the present, reminding me that I was free to live this moment for myself.

As August drew to a close, I stepped into a new chapter: a new school year and a new internship. This internship has been a kind of saving grace for me, a place where I feel a renewed sense of purpose. Walking into my own office every day and being given responsibilities that actually mean something makes each day fly by. My time is filled with meaningful work, with creativity, with connection, and with people who make me feel like I'm doing something worthwhile. I've started to see my strengths again and trust that I have something valuable to offer.

And then, on September 6, came my brother's wedding. Alyssa was my date, and everything about that day felt... right. I'd worried, initially, about how I'd feel, attending Sophie and Nick's wedding without someone by my side, especially in the wake of everything that's happened. But with Alyssa there, it didn't feel like anything was missing. The ceremony was beautiful, flawless in a way that felt genuine. As I watched my brother say his vows, I was overwhelmed by this sense of joy for him, for the love he's found, a love that feels deep and true.

Standing there, in that celebration of love and commitment, I felt a strange sense of peace, as if everything that had happened was meant to lead me to this moment. For the first time, I wasn't longing for something or someone else. I wasn't wishing Austin was there, or anyone else, for that matter. Instead, I was grateful—for my family, for Alyssa, for the chance to be truly present, no longer weighed down by the hurt of what I'd left behind. It was a day to celebrate love, and in a small, quiet way, it felt like a celebration of my own journey, too.

### Tuesday, September 24, 2024

*The past few months have been like a slow, gentle shift—a season of change that's brought me a new kind of happiness. It feels like I'm settling into a routine that gives me a sense of balance and accomplishment I didn't realize I needed. Each day seems a little fuller, a little brighter, and I'm finally feeling like myself again.*

*Starting this internship has given me something to look forward to each morning. I walk in, ready to take on new tasks, and I leave each day feeling like I'm actually making a difference. I feel purposeful in a way that makes everything else seem to fall into place a little easier. It's amazing how having a focus can shift my entire outlook like there's something solid and real to hold on to.*

*This past month especially, I've noticed how much lighter I feel. There's more laughter and more moments where I catch myself smiling without realizing it. I'm finding a rhythm in life that feels right. I'm even starting to feel that sense of calm when I think about what's ahead—less anxiety about what's behind me, less of wishing things were different.*

*I'm grateful for this quiet kind of happiness, the kind that sneaks up on me when I'm least expecting it. It's a good place to be.*

*Chapter*

# 28

# Return to Sender

Austin has been on my mind more often lately. Not in the way he used to be, when memories of him would make my heart ache and my stomach twists with longing. This was different. He lingered like a ghost, drifting through my thoughts when I least expected it. Maybe it was the holiday season approaching, but I found myself wondering about him—what he was doing, how he was feeling, and if he ever thought of me, too. The questions didn't sting like they once did, but they still left me unsettled.

Tonight, the weight of it all became too much, I couldn't focus on anything, and my mind was going a mile a minute. I grabbed my keys and headed out, needing the clarity that only an open road could bring. The cool autumn air wrapped around me as I drove. The rhythmic hum of the engine and the glow of the sun were my only companions. The streets were quiet, my thoughts swirled with every turn of the wheel, memories of us playing like a silent film in my mind.

I ended up at the overlook, a place we'd gone to once on a whim. It had been summer then, the air thick with warmth, and the sky streaked with shades of orange and pink as the sun dipped below the horizon.

Tonight, the same view was shrouded in a quiet, cool stillness; the stars scattered like tiny shards of light across the inky black sky. I parked the car, opened the sunroof, leaned back in my seat, and let out a long, steady breath.

I pulled out my journal, the one that had become my sanctuary in the months since we ended. The pages were filled with my thoughts, my pain, and my hopes for a future where his name no longer lingered in my chest. As I reread each entry, I felt the pain of every word slowly lifting from me, as if the weight of those emotions was being released with each sentence. It was a cathartic experience, allowing me to reflect on the struggles I had faced. Each carefully chosen phrase carried memories and feelings I had almost forgotten. The act of revisiting those moments helped me process them, transforming the raw emotions into something more manageable. With every word, I felt lighter and more liberated, as if I was shedding layers of sorrow and confusion I had carried for far too long. Tonight, I turned to a fresh page and let the words pour out.

### Friday, October 25, 2024

*Austin,*

*I don't know if I'll ever say these words out loud, but I need to write them, if only for myself. There's so much I've carried with me since the day we met—the good, the bad, and everything in between. Tonight, as I sit here with nothing but the soft hum of the world around me, I feel ready to let it all out.*

*I want to start with gratitude. For all the ways you made me smile, for the times you held me close when I felt like the world was crumbling. You showed me what it felt like to be loved, even if it wasn't always the love I deserved. I'll never forget the nights we stayed up talking about our dreams, our fears, and the future we thought we'd share. You made me believe in something I didn't think I could have, and for that, I'll always be thankful.*

*But gratitude can't erase the hurt. There were cracks in our foundation from the start—small fractures I tried to ignore, telling myself they didn't matter. But they did. Every time your words felt distant, or your actions didn't match your promises, those cracks deepened. I trusted you with my heart, my vulnerabilities, and my dreams, and sometimes, it felt like you didn't even see them. The lies, the betrayals, the way you made me feel like I was never enough—those are the memories that linger, the ones that took me so long to let go of.*

*I never wanted anything but the best for you and to see that wonderful smile of yours as much as possible. And for that, I don't seek revenge. I was always kind to you. I loved you unconditionally, and I always made sure you were safe and felt heard. Your actions, though, were a reflection of who you are, not of me. Even though you knew what you were doing to me was wrong, I never had it in me to do the same to you. That's something you'll have to carry, even if you never admit it. And you'll always have to live with the fact that when it mattered the most, you couldn't man up.*

*I've spent countless nights replaying the moments that broke us, wondering if I could've done something different, been someone different, to make us work. But now, I see it wasn't my job to hold us together. Love isn't about losing yourself to keep someone else. It's about standing side by side, equal and whole, and building something together. And while we didn't have that, I know now that I can—with someone who sees me for all that I am and chooses me, and only me, with the truest intentions.*

*I used to think closure would come from you—an apology, an explanation, something to make sense of it all. But closure isn't something you can give me. It's something I've had to find within myself.*

*Tonight, as I write this, I feel like I've finally found it. I'm letting go of the anger, the pain, the love I held onto for so long. I'm leaving it here, in these words, so it no longer weighs me down.*

*I wish you well, Austin. I hope you find the happiness you're searching for. And I hope one day, I do, too—in a way that feels steady, true, and unshakeable.*

*Goodbye.*

*Lily*

~ ~ ~

As I finished writing, tears blurred my vision, but they felt different this time. They weren't tears of heartbreak or longing; they were tears of release. I closed the journal and set it on the passenger seat, leaning back to look out at the stars. The weight I'd been carrying for so long felt lighter now, as if putting it into words had loosened its grip on me.

The night was still, the world quiet around me, and for the first time in what felt like forever, my heart felt quiet, too. I didn't know what the future held, but I knew this: I was ready to face it. With one last deep breath, I started the car, the soft rumble of the engine breaking the silence, and pulled back onto the road. The journey wasn't over, but tonight, I'd taken a step forward. And that was enough.

*Chapter*

## 29

# Winter's Beginning

Winter is settling in, wrapping the world in its quiet, reflective chill. I find myself feeling a strange kind of warmth in the cold, as though the season itself is urging me to shed the remnants of what once was, to step fully into a new beginning.

It's strange, looking back now, to think that I once believed love alone could save us. There was a time when I thought those nights we spent together—those rare moments when everything felt like it might fall into place—were enough to carry us through anything. But in the end, they were just moments, fleeting and fragile. Beautiful, yes, but never enough.

I wanted to be the one who could show him a better way, someone whose loyalty and patience could make up for his indifference. But slowly, painfully, I realized that love, on its own, couldn't bear the weight of everything we lacked. Deep down, I knew this truth all along; it just took time to find the courage to listen.

Letting go wasn't one single moment. It wasn't a dramatic goodbye or a clean break. It was a gradual process, a quiet acceptance that grew as I noticed the tiny fractures—each one a reminder that he couldn't meet me where I needed to be met. With each disappointment, each broken promise, I began to understand what love truly is: not just the thrill or the idea of "forever," but the choice to nurture, protect, and honor someone's heart.

For so long, I thought my loyalty would be enough to counteract his disloyalty, but loyalty that demands self-sacrifice turns heavy and bitter, slowly eroding the very foundation of who you are until there's nothing left to give—not to them, and not to yourself. The sacrifices I made, which I thought would bring us closer, only deepened the divide. It's a painful realization, but I've learned that for love to thrive, there must be balance. Loyalty should enhance connection, not diminish your happiness or sense of self.

I wanted so badly for him to show up for me, to see me fully, but love doesn't grow in the shadows. I deserved more than someone I had to convince of my worth. Love isn't meant to be something we cling to in desperation. Sometimes, the bravest thing you can do is let go.

Through this journey, I've found a strength within myself that I never knew existed. Healing didn't come from erasing the past but from confronting it. Every tear, sleepless night, and moment of doubt has shaped me into someone who understands her worth—someone who demands respect and knows that real love builds you up, not tears you apart.

This ending is more than just an ending. It's a beginning. It's a call to rebuild, to rediscover who I am outside of the person I was with him. I've had to release the guilt, the shame, the anger, and the regret. Piece by piece, I'm reclaiming the parts of myself I'd given away. Healing, I've realized, isn't a destination; it's an ongoing journey, a constant unfolding.

As I reflect, there's something I want to share with you. My experience felt so unique at the time, like no one could possibly understand the weight of what I was carrying. I found myself comparing my relationship to others, justifying staying by thinking, *"Well, at least he never physically cheated on me."* I see now how those comparisons kept me trapped, holding on to a love that wasn't truly serving me.

Every relationship has its challenges, and I still believe true love is worth fighting for. But never at the expense of your basic needs. In any relationship—romantic, platonic, or familial—you should never lower your standards for the respect and care you deserve. Love, in its truest form, is rooted in mutual respect. Without it, there is no foundation to build on.

So, if you find yourself in a situation like mine—whether you're still in it, just stepping away, or trying to heal—know this: you *will* make it through. It won't be easy, and it will take strength you didn't know you had, but the first step is choosing yourself.

Looking back now, I feel a strange gratitude for every hurt, every lesson carved into my heart. They've shown me how to trust myself, honor my boundaries, and demand the respect I once hoped would be freely given. This journey has been about so much more than love—it's been about reclaiming my voice, my happiness, and my power.

As I close this chapter of my life, I feel lighter, stronger, and free. I know now that I am worthy of a love that lifts me up, one that doesn't leave me questioning my worth. And perhaps the greatest lesson of all is this: I don't need someone else to complete my story. I am whole on my own.

As the first winter snowflakes begin to fall, I'm ready—ready for whatever comes next, ready to embrace the unknown, knowing that everything I need is already within me.

### Sunday, December 15, 2024

*Today, there's a stillness within me—a calm I've fought hard to find. As I sit here, looking back, I can feel the weight of the past lifting. I see those memories for what they are now: stories that brought me to this very moment, not scars to hold me back.*

*For the longest time, I thought I needed to be loved to feel whole. But now, I realize that the love I needed most was my own, and it took losing someone I thought was everything, to find it. I was always enough. It just took leaving to see that, to remember what I deserve, and to promise myself I'll never settle for less again.*

*There were days when I felt utterly shattered, as if I would never experience real joy again. But now, there's a flicker of something new—hope. Not the naive kind that believed in fairy tales, but the kind that trusts in my own strength, my own worth, my own journey. I've learned that being alone isn't a void to fill but a space to breathe, to heal, and to grow.*

*I hope that one day, the butterflies return to my stomach, but this time for someone who makes me feel safe, never having to feel that gut feeling he caused me ever again. I want the kind of love that feels light, that doesn't leave me questioning.*

*I don't know where life will take me next, but I'm finally okay with that. For the first time, I'm looking forward without needing someone else to be waiting on the other side. I'm ready for love, but not the kind that completes me—the kind that celebrates who I already am.*

*So here's to me, to everything I've endured and everything I'm becoming. Here's to a future where I'm whole, where I'm happy, and where, finally, I am free.*

# Reflections & Gratitude

Writing this memoir has been a journey of healing, resilience, and self-discovery. Reflecting on the heartache, the joy, and the lessons that have shaped me has allowed me to confront difficult truths and reclaim my strength. My hope is that these pages resonate with anyone who has ever felt the weight of lost love or the transformative power of choosing oneself.

To my family—your unwavering love and understanding kept me anchored through the hardest times. Thank you for standing by me as I stumbled, learned, and grew. To my parents, who gave me a safe space to break down and rebuild, and to my brother, Chris, my steady rock, who reminded me of my strength just by being there—I am endlessly grateful.

To my extended family, even from afar, your support has meant more than words can express. Your presence in my life, your words of encouragement, and your belief in me have been a constant source of comfort, reminding me that I am never truly alone on this journey.

To my closest friends, my chosen sisters, who listened without judgment, lifted me up, and reminded me of my worth when I struggled to see it—you each brought light when I needed it most. Alexis, for your shoulder to cry on and your honesty; you stood by me when I couldn't stand on my own. Ally, for your unyielding support, our sisterhood, and your kindness. Danielle, for the laughter and memories that reminded me of life's beauty, even in my darkest days.

And finally, to every person who reads this memoir—thank you. It is a vulnerable act to share one's life so openly, but if my story can serve as a small light, a comfort, or a moment of reflection, then it has done more than I could have hoped. Healing isn't always easy, but it's always within reach. In sharing this journey, I find myself a little closer to peace, and I hope it brings you closer to yours.

*With Love, Olivia*

www.ingramcontent.com/pod-product-compliance
Lightning Source LLC
Chambersburg PA
CBHW051834040426

42447CB00006B/532